Fortress of the Heart...

the story of Anna

Anna Coleman

SHIRLEY COLEMAN-WELLS

Shirley Coleman-Wells

Hughes Henshaw Publications
Denver, Colorado

Copyright © 1997 by Shirley Coleman-Wells

Cover design by Lauren McAdam

All rights reserved, including the right to reproduce this work in any form whatsoever, without permission in writing from the publisher, except for brief passages in connection with a review.

For information write:

Hughes Henshaw Publications
7196 West Fourth Avenue
Lakewood, Colorado 80226-1642

Or call: (303) 237-5905
FAX: (303) 233-6545
email: hugheshens@aol.com
Web site: http://www.hugheshenshaw.com

If you are unable to order this book from your local booksellers, you may order directly from the publisher. Quantity discounts are available.

Library of Congress Catalog Number: 98-36397

ISBN 0-9617223-2-0

Type Font: Baskerville

Printed in Canada

Dedication

This book is for my mother, Anna. I thank you for your life, your love and your wisdom. And I thank you for the mid-mornings, when I was four years old and the others had left for school, when you would read poetry to me. I know I write my words today because of those times. I love you.

I thank my daddy, who sternly and unknowingly molded me to be strong, free and outspoken. You are a legacy in itself and I salute you. I carry both your name and the *look* proudly. I love you and miss you.

To my children Tami and Traci, I love you. You have grown to be beautiful, special young ladies and you have my devotion. You've earned it. I love you.

To my granddaughters, Victoria and Brea, you are my world. You comfort me and make me laugh, and you are my reason for living. I love you, I love you.

To my sisters and brothers, I both applaud and thank you for trying, in your many different ways to understand me. Mom's book has brought us much closer together and I love you all.

To Aunt Essie, who lent her life, her knowledge and her laughter to this book. I miss you. You filled in a lot of the gaps. I love you.

To my many nieces, nephews, and cousins, please remember to take just a little of your time to acknowledge Nanny, for she is truly a work of art.

To Karen Lee Banks, my best friend in this world, who with craziness and laughter saw me through all the bad times. I will always and forever thank you for facing me and smiling in my face, rather than talking out of both sides of your mouth behind my back. I love you, my best friend, and know that all my successes are your successes.

To Vionette Kearney, although you have gained your wings, there's not a day that you are not in my heart. I love you my distant friend, and I still remember our dreams. I hope you are proud of me.

Francisco Colon, you will eternally be my friend for you've hung right in there, never judging, always consoling and ever listening. I love you my compadre. We started on this book journey a long time ago and I hope you're there when all is said and done. Our Tushkin series is right around the corner.

Acknowledgments

I acknowledge and honor the following teachers who, many years ago, took time to encouraged me to be the best I could be and to believe in myself. They were both dedicated and instilled a sense of excitement within me that continues to inspire me today. You've been part of my decision to be a writer. I salute you Mrs. Suzanne Wilson and Mr. Edward Holmes.

I'd also like to extend a special thanks to my sister, Esther. From day one she was there—typing everything, sending out letters and talking to me even when nothing was going on. I love you and thank you.

I am indebted to Daphna Moore for her faith and confidence in me. I'm so grateful she chose to believe in my abilities as a writer, and for pushing this project to the top. I'm proud to call you my friend.

Lola, I am fortunate to have you in my life and for being everything I aspire to be. Never leave.

Finally, I feel gratitude for my fellow, who for thirty years has quietly guided and steered me down love's pathway. I love you for knowing when to let me go, and better yet, when to come back. I thank you for loving me through all our secrets, and my *nutty trips*, as well as my fears. Those who have fleetingly passed through our lives will never understand us because they have merely been the players. We are the real stars. I love you.

Henry McBride stands against the railing of the small *River Boat*, focusing on the waters of the Mississippi. A slight wind sends a breeze off the water as the boat tilts gently side to side. He thinks of his life—calm, turbulent, then calm like the river, as you almost wait for the story to begin again. A tall black man, with deep-set eyes; he's handsome by any standards. Dark curly hair encases a slim face, boned to perfection, stern, yet with soft eyes.

Stooping to pick up some loose pebbles underfoot, he looks at his hands. They're worn and strong, but almost unweathered by the foe that has beset the rest of his family. Dropping tiny stones into the water, he watches the ripples spread and blend into the river, as he and his brothers and sisters had been spread through slavery—spread, then blended into the population of unknown faces and names.

So long ago, yet often they were still on his mind, and always in his heart.

As the sun started its decent, Henry closed his eyes. The *River Boat* rocked gently, cradling his thoughts, blotting today as he prayed a silent, hushed prayer.

Dear Jesus, let them all be safe. Let them all be content and happy. Let them know that their labor of life will, one day, be known. Please let them know that I love them.

Henry opened his eyes. The sun had decided to linger, and had cast an orange glow about the sky. It reflected off the water, reminding him of an evening long ago when he was small. It seems he and his brothers, determined to hunt dinner that evening, wandered too far into the woods looking for possum. The more they tried to walk out, the thicker the trees became till they were enveloped in thicket and branches like the long arms of a stalking enemy. Finally they sat down by a huge oak tree to wait. The sun was mid-sky, getting ready to retire, and Henry was so afraid that it would set. Then came the footsteps, the crackling of branches, and the clearing of limbs. There was Pa, with a worried look—a stiff swatting, and a reprimand.

"A lickin' never felt so good," thought Henry, as his father lifted the boys up and headed home.

The boat rocked. Henry thought of a Christmas when their only present was a manger of the baby Jesus. His Pa had to make it of birch bark and displayed it proudly in front of the small tree, adorned only with bits of paper and cotton. He remembered the beautiful face that his mother had painted on the baby with mud and red clay, and how relieved he was, to peek in the tiny manger and find that baby Jesus was black. He remembered what a wonderful Christmas it had been, sitting there eating biscuits and gravy with his family, singing the carols, and talking of Jesus' birth. Looking at the black baby in the manger with tattered clothes, Henry felt warm. Even though his thin shirt and pants were ragged, he felt warm, and likened himself to the baby somehow.

The winds picked up, sending a cool mist into the air, like an un-seen vapor. It felt good on Henry's face, as he continued his journey into yesterday. His mind settled on a cold day in winter when the men came and took them all to town. Standing in the cold street, like tainted meat, they were all sold like cattle one by one. He watched his brother struggle as they put him in a wagon, and his little sister's face as they put her in another.

"Don't cry!" he thought. "Please don't cry!" But he knew this was forever. He watched his mother and father being led in another direction, and he knew he'd never see them again.

Henry remembered thinking, "This must be a dream." But he knew that dreams don't pierce your heart so. Years later, word had it, his Ma and Pa had died. He remembered breathing a sigh of relief.

So wrapped in thought was Henry that he didn't notice a few of the passengers milling near-by, nor did he hear the low voice of Jake Buchanan.

"Henry, are you all right? Are you okay?" Henry blinked and looked over his shoulder. It was then that he was aware of the several white passengers who had gathered.

"I'm all right," he said. "Just a little deep in thought."

Jake paused and spoke softly to his friend.

"Of the thoughts that we've talked about so often?" he asked.

Henry's silence was his answer.

Just then a small white woman spoke up. Her voice was squeaky and Henry wanted to laugh because she was so ugly, and her bonnet had tilted from the winds.

"You allow your boy to think?" She sneered at Jake, amid the laughter and stares from the small crowd.

Jake was quiet. He cleared his throat, more from habit than necessity, and looked at them squarely.

"I don't allow this *man* anything," he said. "No need to. See, he's a free man. His wishes and his thoughts are his own."

The crowd was still, having been reduced to silence. They stood there mute, like dime store mannequins, shocked at such talk from a white man. Then they slowly walked away, muttering, looking back, and shaking their heads.

Henry turned to Jake nodding his appreciation. He looked at the clear blue eyes and the face that for so long he has called—friend. He watched Jake blow smoke circles with his pipe, his once sun-blonde hair now tinged with gray. Their eyes met, and Jake again cleared his throat, facing Henry.

"Those weren't just words," he said. "I mean 'um Henry. I told you long ago that I have no slaves, just people who help me out."

Patting Henry's shoulder, Jake again faced the water, slipping into silence—his mind filled with the dusk and his thoughts.

Jake recalled the day his father had brought Henry home. He was thin, but handsome with soft eyes. He'd said he got Henry real cheap cause he was so tall and skinny. Both boys were eight, and Jake was pleased. Maybe this meant that he wouldn't have to play with his sister anymore.

"Thanks Pa," he had yelled out loud, only to be rebuked by his father.

"The boy's a slave!" his father boomed. "He's no friend! I brought him here to work, to do chores. Now take him out back to the shed so old Pete can show him what to do!"

Jake glanced at his mother, but knew she wouldn't speak up. She never spoke up much, just sat in her room a lot. Motioning to Henry, he took him across the grounds to the shed. Both boys were silent, and Jake wondered how his father could make a human a slave.

For the next few months the boys stayed clear of each other. Jake knew his Father was mostly all wind, but he wanted the air to settle a bit. He wanted Henry to have time to adjust to these new surroundings. Henry remained quiet, his mind always so far away, almost distant, his eyes sad.

One day when Jake's father went to town, Jake hung on the fence watching Henry chop weeds. Leaning over the fence, he yelled to Henry. Henry looked up—his child eyes serious—then slowly walked to the fence, facing the small boy with blonde tussled hair and blue eyes. No one spoke.

Finally Jake said shyly, "Are you any good with animals?"

"I'm fair," said Henry. Again the silence.

"Well," Jake continued. "I got this bird that I found yesterday, and he's hurt— real bad. His wings all scrunched, and I thought maybe you'd like to help me fix him up!"

Henry looked down at the small bird, which lay by Jake's feet. He reached through the fence, touching its feathers, smoothing its wing.

Jake went on. "He could be our pet, and we can meet every day to feed and water him, and put sticks on his wing—that is if you want to?"

Henry looked up.

"Your Pa won't take a liken' to that," he said, a small flicker of hope, dimming.

"So what?" said Jake. "My Pa don't take a liken' to much, `cept money. Besides, he'll never know. We'll meet here every night at ten o'clock and bring some water and a dish. I'll even tear up one of my sister's new petticoats for cloth for the nest and the splint. Her best petticoat, too," he laughed—the tension over.

"And I'll bring some of the chicken feed from old Pete," laughed Henry. "That way the bird will have plenty to eat."

"Then it's a deal," said Jake, sticking out his hand to Henry, who shook it with a grin. "Why, you don't feel no different than I do," said Jake in surprise as both boys settled on opposite sides of the fence.

They had great plans for that bird. He was gonna grow up and be a giant eagle, and take them out over the seas. They would each ride a wing, be adventurers, and wherever there was sunken treasure, the big bird would swoop down, scoop it up, and soar into the sky with its big wings spread into eternity. But Jake's mother called, shattering their fantasy.

"It must be dinner time," he said as he headed out over the fields to the big house. "Don't forget, meet me here at ten o'clock!" he yelled back.

"Ten o'clock,"said Henry as he ran back to his weedin'. At ten o'clock Henry sat by the fence waiting. The night was still and warm as he nestled in the grass, his eyes closed, listening to the sounds. Crickets rubbed their tune to the low of the cows and pigs off in the distance. An owl attempted Alto, cutting in oddly, off beat. Even though he had no watch, Henry knew that it was getting late—way past ten. He stroked the small bird, feeling dejected, thinking what a fool he had been. How dare he presume that the boy would show up.

Off in the distance a figure made its way across the pasture to the fence. Henry held his breath, just knowing it was Mr. Buchanan. He closed his eyes, trying to evaporate into the night. But as the figure neared, he saw that it was too small to be Mr. Buchanan. It was Jake. He ran up puffing and spewing apologies. It seems his sister had gotten sick. His folks were tending her and he couldn't get to the petticoat until they got settled.

"It's after eleven o'clock. Let's get to work." said Jake.

Henry agreed, thinking, "He came! He really came."

The two boys set to task, building a rickety nest and filling it with the seed and water. After gathering a small pile of twigs, they tore the frilly petticoat in strips, then attached the splint to the bird's wing. It fluttered just slightly, its quick breath rapid, but the boys assumed this was because it had been through such an ordeal. Surely he would be all right now, for he was in such good care. Putting the bird in its nest, they settled back against the fence, and listened to the sounds of the night.

"My Pa says you people aren't like us," said Jake. "He says you don't act or think or even feel like us. But I don't really see no difference, 'cept you're darker than I am. Is that bad?"

But Henry didn't answer. He sat looking at the heavens, the stars blinking a code of invitation. How he wished that one would fall and envelop him with its light, lifting him into the skies. How he wished that he could hover above the world, and look down at the hate that could not touch him so far above. He cried. He cried in quiet muffled tones, thinking of that cold day in front of the store when all that he'd loved was so cruelly taken from him. He was angry for crying in front of an almost stranger, yet the tears came and came, like a seasonal rain, able to stop only at the sun. So he let it rain, oblivious to the boy who sat helpless, knowing his very being was a part of this misery.

Jake cried some too, for somehow inside he could almost feel Henry's pain. They were two small boys, huddled against the night, in a world that was destined not to understand. He put his arm around Henry, wondering how it would feel to be taken from his own family. He whispered, "I'll be your friend till I die. I promise." His words seemed to calm Henry, and the two boys sat 'til dawn.

And such were their lives from then on. Every day when Jake got home from school he took Henry out back of the shed to teach him what he'd learned that day. Henry wasn't allowed to go to school, so Jake saw to it that he learned to read and write and talk properly. In return, Henry taught Jake how to play the guitar and harmonica. Mr. Buchanan left them alone after awhile. Besides, he had to admit that Henry was a good boy. Henry, on the other hand, was careful to be kind and polite—always calling Jake *Mr. Buchanan* in front of others.

Both men grew up straight and handsome. At nineteen, Henry married Esther, a slim pretty woman, with big eyes and brown skin. Jake went to the wedding out back, giving his friend away, and laughing as Henry fell trying to jump the wedding brooms. Esther and Henry moved to a small cabin out back of the big house. A few months later Jake married Millie, a small frail woman with dark hair. Henry wasn't allowed at the wedding, but Jake saw to it that he and Esther got some of the refreshments, afterwards.

Millie, knowing Jake's pact with Henry, was as friendly as possible, times being what they were. Sometimes she knitted small doilies or dishtowels for Esther, who accepted them as if they were laced with gold. Pa Buchanan had shifted a lot of important matters to his son which kept him busy, but Jake often talked to Henry about the big eagle that was to have taken them away in search of adventure.

Autumn was about them, its leaves dotting the trees like a patchwork quilt. Esther and Henry had a baby daughter they named Nancy. She was fat and brown, with Esther's eyes and a quick smile.

The last week or so Jake had been spending a lot of time in town. Henry never questioned this as Jake had become a businessman of sorts. Besides, Henry was too busy with the livestock and the cotton. There was a lot of work to do, a lot to oversee.

One day Jake came back from town, excited, in a hurry. He rushed into the house calling for his father, and found him in the study, sitting behind his large oak desk. Old man Buchanan peered over his glasses, visibly agitated at the interruption. Jake cleared his throat, shifting from one foot to the other, then started.

"Sir," he said, "Pardon the intrusion, but I've been in town the last few days and you wouldn't believe all that's going on. Pa, there's these new boats, only these boats are like floating cabins with food. Passengers pay a fare to ride up and down the Mississippi on them, plus they carry cargo up the river. They're called *River Boats* and Pa, I want to buy one to set up a trade of my own. I could get in on the ground floor if I buy now, and there's a good profit in it. In a few years the boat will more than pay for itself."

Mr. Buchanan sat back in his chair. He was silent for what seemed like an eternity, but obviously thinking the matter over carefully.

Finally he spoke.

"You say there's profit in this?"

Another pause.

"Well, I never was one to stand in the way of profit. Buy the boat."

Jake sighed in relief, but, as he headed towards the door, he stopped.

"Pa, there's one more thing," he said, his voice low, nervous.

"I want you to give me Henry McBride's papers and all. I want you to sign him over to me so we can run the *River Boat* together."

He faced his father and waited for his reply, feeling small beads of sweat on his brow.

"He's a good man, Pa," he finished. "I'll need his help to run so big a boat."

The old man looked deep into his son's eyes. They were strong now, unlike the impish boy who snuck behind the shed to read to Henry.

"We'll talk after dinner," he said. "Meet me in the drawing room."

At dinner Jake picked at his food. With it half eaten, he excused himself, going to the drawing room to wait. Sitting in a comfortable chair, he was excited, afraid but excited, sorta like the time he had ditched school for three days to go fishing with Henry. And they would have gotten away with it too, if his sister hadn't told. But boy did they get back at her. It probably took her three weeks to get all the sorghum out of her hair. He smiled. Yes, him and Henry had done it all; against fierce opposition, they'd managed to remain friends. He thought about his promise to Henry by the fence. He thought about their pact to become pirates. "Well, maybe we won't be pirates," he thought. "Maybe we won't sail the high seas for sunken treasure, but we could run the *River Boat* together along the Mississippi."

The door opened. His father came in leaning on a cane, walking slowly. He poured two brandies, handed one to Jake, and sat facing him. Reaching in his coat pocket he handed Jake some yellowed papers.

"He's yours," he said. "Now leave me."

Jake jumped up, his boyish vigor apparent. Then thanking his father, he raced down the stairs, and out back to Henry's cabin.

Jake knocked feverishly at Henry's door. Henry opened it, puzzled, wondering who died. Jake peeked in at Esther, who was busy putting baby Nancy to sleep, and whispered, "Come out to the fence, Henry. I gotta tell you something."

Henry grabbed his shirt and followed Jake to the fence. During the walk he watched Jake half running ahead of him, and thought about how intense he still got about things, just like when they were children. He remembered how excited he'd been about the tiny bird, even though it died a week later.

At the fence Jake grabbed Henry's shoulder. His blue eyes sparkled and danced as if someone hid in the bushes, playing a minuet.

"Henry," he said, "I guess you've noticed that I've been in and out of town a lot these last few weeks? Well, I've bought a golden eagle, a huge bird bent on adventure, with a treasure all its own."

Henry looked at his friend in silence.

"He's drunk," he thought. "He's dipped in the brandy a tad too much."

But Jake went on.

"Henry, I bought a river boat. A huge floating house that will take people up and down the Mississippi."

He went on to explain its every virtue, and when he stopped, Henry spoke up.

"Sounds good Jake," he said. "Sounds real good."

But inside he felt sad, dejected, a small ache mustering that he felt guilty for. It seemed like a friendship was ending, like a pact had been severed—and he was ashamed of himself, ashamed of not being happier for Jake, ashamed of feeling sorry for himself. But after all, Jake was a white man, and owed him nothing. How dare he believe that they would remain friends forever. How selfish. He took Jake's hands in his, his dark eyes soft, his heart warming.

"I'm honestly happy for you Jake," he said. And he meant it.

Jake stood looking at Henry, the same smile on his face.

"But listen to this," he said. "You don't belong to my Pa anymore. Just today he gave you to me. Henry, from this day on you're a free man, and I'm giving you your freedom. Won't you come with me on the *River Boat*? Esther and Nancy will be fine right here. Millie will see to them. Henry, I couldn't possibly go off on that eagle without you. This is what we've been wanting since we were children—to soar, to be free."

Henry stared at the spot where they had buried the bird, so many years before.

"Free!" he thought. I'm free."

Then grabbing Jake, the two men embraced, laughing, jumping, and tearing up the yellow papers, tossing them defiantly into the night.

The *River Boat* rocked gently and the sun had set now, as both men continued to appreciate the water, the quiet, and the memories. It was Henry who brought Jake back to reality.

"I'm going down to check the steam room," he said softly, almost in apology for breaking the silence.

Jake's eyes seemed far away, wrapped in thought of times long past. Henry spoke up again, this time nudging Jake to attention.

"I've been thinking a lot lately," he said. "For some time now I've known that our *River Boat* runs have been slippin', and I know it's because of me. A lot of white folk ain't like you Jake, and they don't take a liken' to me havin' any pull around here. They laugh behind your back. They call you a fool. A black man, workin' alongside a white man? Well, they're not ready for it. I doubt if they'll ever be. It's funny now days, how if a man has a heart, he's a fool. We've run this *River Boat* for some twenty odd years now, and every day of `um I've felt like I've held you back, stopped you from being as well off as you could be."

Jake looked up. He crammed more tobacco in his pipe, and spoke clearly.

"Remember when we were children Henry, and the Johnson boys were menacing me down by the old water hole? Why, they'd of drown me for sure if you hadn't come along. You just snuck right up and beat the snot out of 'um. Course, I helped too after I got my pants back on. Man, they sure were whoopin and hollerin. And my Pa, well, he stood right up for you again' the sheriff. Pa actually hid you for six months. Little did he know that we'd really stole them boys new shoes and filled 'um with tar." Both men laughed out loud.

"Yes, we've been through a lot Henry," Jake went on. "You've been closer to me than any man I know. Just look at us, we're both close to fifty, and we've run this boat up and down this Mississippi for quit a spell now. So what if our passengers have slacked up some, we've had fun haven't we?" We soared this golden bird, just like we said we would, city after city. Grantin' our sunken treasure turned out to be cargo, but it's only cargo if we see it that way. It's been a good life Henry, don't you think?"

Henry smiled.

"You're still such a dreamer," he said, and reached into his pocket for a match for Jake's' pipe.

"Keep the whole match box," he said. "You never were one to carry a light. Now I'm going down to check on the steam room."

"Oh, and Jake," he said back over his shoulder, "Life's been just fine."

Jake lit his pipe, blowing small whiffs like miniature clouds into the night. The *River Boat* was quiet now, as the passengers ate their evening meal. It's funny how they didn't seem to mind a black cook. They even preferred it. He thought about how Henry always said those white folks cookin' was too clear.

Before he went to dinner, Henry came back on deck to tell Jake everything was running smooth.

"Eat with me tonight, Henry, "Jake said, clearing his throat. "I have something to talk to you about. I had the cook fix up a mess of chitlins and greens, and a mince meat pie."

Henry frowned. "Now man, you know I wasn't never too much on chitlins. To me, they smell like dirty feet."

"You're right, said Jake. "I always liked `um more than you. But come on down anyway. I'll have the cook bring in some slices of ham, to go with your greens and pie."

"Speakin' of mince pie," said Henry. "Remember how we used to steal `um when we were little and take 'um out by the fence, then blame it on William, and they'd beat the fire out of him? You know I bet poor William got beat every Saturday night."

They laughed. Boyish laughs about yesterday. Remembering always seemed to take the edge off of things. This was when they were at their best—talking and staring out over the Mississippi.

The rich aromas of hot food met Henry as he entered Jake's cabin. The *River Boat* was cool at night, the wood leaving a damp smell in the air. Everything smelt so good, for Henry hadn't realized how hungry he was. Even the chitlins could have been inviting, with the help of a stiff drink!

Both men set to their meal, and not much was said until they cut the mince pie.

"Sure don't taste like my Ma's," drawled Henry. "But it's tasty, real tasty."

Jake reached for his pipe and tobacco pouch. Settling back in his chair, he watched as Henry cut another piece of pie. Slowly he spoke, as if choosing his words, or maybe just the right time to say them.

"We're not young men anymore, Henry," he started. "We both got wives, you've got children, and the river running has taken up a lot of our time."

Jake paused, searching around on the table for a match.

"Henry, I've been thinkin' of settling myself some, givin' up the *River Boat*. It comes a time when a man needs his family about him. Don't you miss Esther and the children?"

Henry nodded. He pictured his children and Esther's smile, but the *River Boat* had been such a big part of his life that he wasn't quite sure what Jake's announcement meant for him or his family. He felt like he did that day twenty some years ago when Jake first told him he was buying the boat. He felt suddenly tense, afraid, for the *River Boat* had afforded him a certain degree of freedom—freedom that he wasn't sure he could maintain on land. It was silent, and the noise was piercing as Henry scooted back his chair.

"I'll be back," he said. "I need to walk and think a spell." Then heading toward the door, he asked, "Would this make you happy?" Jake nodded, as Henry threw him a box of matches, closing the door behind him.

The deck was deserted, as all the passengers had retired. Henry stood against the railing, listening to the rudder gently slapping the cool water. This sound had lulled him to sleep for so many nights. He looked out over the waters that seemed to cut him off from the starkness of the real world. He thought of Esther, of how strong and patient she was. Of how often he'd been gone. The children were gettin' on up now, and Esther had done most of their rearing. Granted, he'd been there for all the important times and holidays, and they'd all lived pretty well, but he knew it wasn't enough. They needed him.

"Maybe it's time," he sighed out loud. "Maybe it's time to get a plot of land somewhere, and farm."

A wave splashed the sides of the boat. Gulls cried out, and the coolness of the wind off the water chilled Henry through his thin shirt. Walking down the steps to his small cabin, he stretched out on the bunk, allowing his mind to wander. Closing his eyes, he saw Esther clearly.

Guess he hadn't realized how much he missed her 'til tonight. He remembered how they'd met at the church in the woods. It wasn't really a fine church or anything like that, just a hut that the black folks had built to pray in. He thought of how beautiful she was—then and now—and of their courtship and small wedding where Jake was best man. It seems Esther always knew when the *River Boat* would dock.

She was there, standing in the doorway of their small cabin—smiling, her hair so black, so soft, always piled on top of her head framing her round face. He thought of how she'd almost died having the last baby, and how she'd refuse to name the babies 'til he was by her side.

"Naw, this hasn't been easy on her," he thought. Even though she hadn't complained, he knew it had to be wearing on her. The years had passed so quickly and he had to admit that, at times, he'd thought of quitting the boat but he hadn't wanted to hurt Jake.

Jake was too tired and smoking too much, coughing too much, and lookin' too tired and weary for his age.

"It's that pipe," thought Henry.

He knew in his heart that if they didn't stop soon, the *River Boat* would begin to lose more than it earned. The bigger, fancier boats had taken most of their passengers, and those who had remained were still too leery of him. Plus, some of their cargo was now being handled by bigger boats as the merchants felt Jake was too easy, too lenient. The few who had stayed with Jake, either out of kindness or pity—were not enough to make the *River Boat* prosper, so Henry knew Jake was right. At dinner he had been feeling selfish, thinking more with his heart than his head.

Looking around the dark cabin, Henry made out shapes on the ceiling. Reaching into the dresser, he groped for the small Bible with the quilted bookmark that Esther had given him. Laying it beside him, he closed his eyes.

"It's time," he thought, as he drifted off to sleep. "I suppose it's time."

Henry woke up, startled, fumbling in the dark for the lantern and his pocket watch, which read one o'clock. Brushing back his hair, he raced for the door, sure that Jake was asleep by now.

After knocking lightly on the door and getting no response, he went inside. Jake still sat upright in his chair, his head nodding, his pipe dangling from his hand.

"This fool man's gonna set the whole boat on fire!" thought Henry as he laid the pipe on the table.

Jake mumbled something about cotton, then opened his eyes, focusing on Henry.

"I was waitin' on you," he said. "Got a match?" Henry lit the pipe, and sat down at the table across from Jake. He studied his face, waiting for him to speak, wanting to apologize for not returning earlier but figuring he'd let Jake have his say. Jake puffed his pipe some, then laid it on the table—the two men looking face to face.

"Often when we'd dock, I'd be pricing houses and land and I finally bought one on the edge of Atlanta. I thought you'd be pleased, but earlier you didn't cater to it too well. I don't know what you were thinkin', but let me tell you what I have in mind. I bought a plantation with big white columns, and huge cotton fields. With Pa, Ma, and my sister gone, you and Millie are all I have left. I figure we can all live together. Grantin', Millie and me, we have no children, but you've got plenty and I figure they need to be tended to. Henry, we're getting too old for the *River Boat* now. Why, them younger men got fancier, bigger boats, with bands and such. Let's go home, Henry. That big bird that's carried us for so long needs to land, needs to nest. Come with me to the plantation."

Henry fidgeted with a tin cup on the table. His ears burned and he was ashamed for once more doubting a friend. Taking Jake's hand, he swallowed hard, amazed at this man he thought he knew.

"Then it's done," he said. "Let's go home."

Putting a box of matches on the table, Henry got up to leave; then he said, "Remember when I fell and twisted my ankle, trying to jump them wedding brooms?"

Jake laughed as Henry closed the door behind him. Then leaning back in his chair, he rested his head against the back, thinking it had been a long day.

The plantation was just as Henry had pictured it—slim white columns framed the porch beset with flowers, and rows of cotton lined the fields, while livestock lolled about the pastures. Chickens scurried noisily out of the way of the men Jake had hired to work, and neat small huts sat out back for the help. The well was positioned near the big house for fresh water, as Millie had insisted she needed fresh water daily for her fineries and hair.

  The two men stood out back near the far fence, Jake smoking his pipe, Henry pushing a stubborn cow back out to pasture. The sun was hot, hot and searing, making their clothes stick like school paste. Henry's two daughters, Nancy and Fanny, were at the big house doing their chores along with their mother. Esther and Nancy did most of the cooking while Fanny, who was the youngest, helped clean and did laundry. He watched his girls hang a bushel of clothes on the line, giggling. Looking out over the cotton field, he watched his sons help tie the huge bales of cotton as they listened to the low hum of a distant song. He didn't see Jim, but Will and Mayo were ever at his side.

Jim was his middle son, and although good-hearted, he tended to be rebellious. Jim would stand his ground right or wrong, which, in their times, could be good for the soul but death to the boy. Looking to the east, he saw clouds of dirt and heard the neigh of a horse laboring against both its stride and whip. He knew it was Jim.

Jim slowed his pace, and trotted up to them—wary. He knew he had no business on the horse in the middle of the day.

"Just trying to break him in, Pa," he said. "This horse is stubborn. Mean! He needs to be tamed some."

Henry looked up at his son. "Broken in or killed?" he asked. "Now get down off of there, and get to your chores—now!" Jim looked at his father for a long minute before moving. Then slowly he got down, looking back as he led the horse to the stable. He patted the horse's silky brown mane, and he thought almost out loud.

"Pa thinks he's free, but it still boils down to us workin' for the white man."

For as kind as Jake had been, Jim could not ignore the fact that he was white. He'd heard the stories from the children on the other plantations. He knew of the cruelty and the pain most of the blacks were suffering. It wasn't so bad for him, but did that make it all right for all the others? A silent rage crept into his mind, into his heart, and angrily he slammed the stable gate, running out over the cotton fields, ignoring his father's call. Henry wished he was more like his brother, Mayo.

Henry watched his son in silence. He knew Jim had a lot pent up inside him, for he'd once known this anger. How often had he burned inside at the obvious, and typical injustices that had beset him in his life? How often had he shaken at the thought of his parents and sisters and brothers, who he'd never see again? How often had he swallowed his grief in despair over a senseless, needless death? "Yes, Jim," he thought to himself. "I've been where you're now, I've been there. And I know I'll be there again. Only the Lord gave me one virtue you're lacking. Patience! Be patient boy, and be strong. Don't let hate consume you or it will do just that, and make you no better than those you hate. You're from a new generation and change is bound to come."

Jake and Henry watched as Jim quickly slung bales of cotton onto the wagon. He was a good boy, defiant, but a strong worker. Henry knew that Jake had been more than fair to them. Sure, Jake made the children do chores, but it was never for more than a few hours at a time . They'd never known the toil that he had known as a boy.

The girls loved to cook, and most days were spent preparing meals with their mother, or cleaning. By mid afternoon all the children gathered for their lessons. Jake insisted they get educated, and Millie jumped at the chance to teach them, as there were no schools nearby. Henry knew, that all considered, they had it good and he said so out loud.

Jake cleared his throat and spoke softly. "Don't fret none, Henry. Your boy Jim, there, is just strong willed. Why he's a lot like me when I was a boy."

And Henry thought back. "You're probably right," he answered.

"Let him be Henry," Jake went on. "These are different times. Let's go back up to the house and get some lemonade. We can sit on the porch and talk a bit."

Henry shook his head, "I think I'll go out to the fields and help with the cotton. But you go on. I'll be up in a spell."

Jake watched as Henry crossed the field. He wondered when his hair had turned so gray. It's funny, but he didn't recall it changing. He wondered when the boys had grown so much taller than they had. He watched as Henry picked the cotton—expertly—stuffing it into the brown gunnysacks that lay scattered throughout the field. He smiled. "Henry never was one to just sit and be idle," he thought, as he walked back to the house—alone.

In the house the women were busy cooking and cleaning. Henry's wife, Esther, and daughter, Nancy, bustled about the steaming pots that cooked on the huge wood stove. Millie dashed in and out, more in the way than anything else. She moved pots that shouldn't have been moved, and stirred what shouldn't have been stirred. Nancy rolled her eyes up at the ceiling.

"Ma!" she wailed. "Miss Millie's getting on my nerves. She can't cook, and when I try to, here she comes with those silly measuring cups. Ma, all you need is a dash of this and a dash of that, and the food tastes fine. If she keeps addin' this grainy stuff to the food it's all gonna taste like grass."

Her mother giggled but told her to be quiet.

"Miss Millie means well," she said. "She tries to help, but she's so frail and not well. I guess she's doing the best she can. Now you mind your manners, and hurry up. We got a lot of things to cook before Hog Killin' Day."

Nancy nodded just as Millie ran back into the room, carrying a huge mound of pink dress.

"Esther!" she fluttered. "Just look at my new pink dress. I stepped on the hem, ripping it four inches across, and the lace tore, and..." Esther stopped her.

"Don't worry none," she said. "I've got a brand new spool of bright pink thread. I'll fix it up in no time."

"Oh, bless you," squeaked Millie. "I'll just put it in your room," she yelled back as she scurried out of the kitchen, the pink dress trailing behind her. Esther stood for a minute, wondering how something so trivial could have been so important. Then after pouring the last batch of corn bread into a greased pan, she headed to her room for the sewing box.

Esther and Henry's quarters were at the rear of the house. They weren't as elaborate as the front, but they were roomy and clean. Sitting on the bed, she looked about her—everything was neat and in its place. This part of the house was cool in the summer as the big oak trees lined the windows. A heavy patchwork quilt covered the bed. It was a bit frayed but it meant more to Esther than anything. Her mother had made and given her this quilt many years before, on the day she married Henry. Her newborn children were wrapped warmly in this quilt. She would, some day, give it to Nancy or Fanny when they married.

Picking up her sewing kit, Esther searched around for the pink thread. She had been saving it to sew the girls some new dresses, but that didn't matter. She'd just sew them in beige, and they'd be just as pretty. As she sewed she looked out of the window. The trees provided a light breeze and Esther welcomed it. She thought of Henry, knowing he was out working the fields in the heat. He'd worked so hard all his life, and she never questioned his reasons—not even when he left to ride the *River Boat* on the Mississippi. Henry was a sound, good man who always seemed to make the right decisions.

Esther put down her needle, and thought of her children. Where had the time gone, for they'd grown so fast. It seemed like only yesterday that Nancy and Fanny were fighting by the shed over an ugly rag doll. Now they were cookin' in the kitchen. The boys had grown up tall and handsome, like Henry. All the children had adjusted well to the plantation through the years. Jim was her only worry. He was so restless, so distant. "But he'll be fine," she reasoned, tossing off anything else as sheer nonsense. "He'll be fine, just like the rest of them." Then picking up her needle again, she set to the huge mound of pink dress, wondering in her mind why anyone would want to wear so much dress anyway.

Dinner time was its normal, noisy self; Millie and Jake sat at the heads of the table, with Esther and Henry alongside. The children sat in a line, minding their manners, and speaking only when spoken to. Millie generally took this time to quiz them on their lessons, to see how much they'd learned that day. The men talked of the plantation, cotton, and the *River Boat*, while Esther generally sat silent listening to her children.

Both families tried to avoid too many black and white issues, but sometimes the slave trade or a black's death would come up. These were always tense times, guilty times, and sad times. Jim often reacted violently, angrily to these subjects, and more than once he had left the table in a rage, only to return with an apology.

But tonight, most of the talk was about Hog Killin' Day. This was some day, a day when it was confirmed which plantation was the best—the fastest. Those hogs had to be killed in record time, then afterwards, a get-together with food and fiddle music. Some of the other plantations were allowed to visit, and for one night, tension was eased. For one night, people laughed and danced, and old men told tall tales. For one night.

"Gotta get up early in the morning with the children," said Henry. "Figure we can get the fields and chores done by ten, to beat that morning sun. Then we can get right to the hog killing. I'm gonna turn in."

Jake watched Henry as he walked the long hallway to his room. He watched him climb the stairs, more slowly now, almost as if feeling his way. He watched Esther and the children clear the table, then retreat. Looking down the long table at his wife, he smiled to himself.

"And just when did she turn so gray?" he wondered as he puffed on his pipe.

Henry awoke instinctively with the first sounds of morning. He sat on the end of the bed, rubbing his eyes and stretching. Esther looked so peaceful, sleeping, that he almost hated to wake her. But this was to be a special day, a busy day. They all had to get an early start.

"Wake up Es," he whispered. "Wake up and rouse the children, while I wash up and dress." Esther got up and headed for the children's rooms. Henry quickly dressed and rushed down the back hall to the door. He raced to the cotton fields, only to be met by Jake at the gate.

"Been up for an hour or so," Jake said. "I got the men up early, instructing them to hurry and eat, and get out to the fields. No sir, no one lagged this morning. We're gonna get all the chores done before that hot sun hits us."

Henry looked surprised. "I sure thought I was the first one up," he said. "Sorry I slept so late."

"You're not late, Henry," Jake laughed. "I'm just early. Well, come on into the kitchen with me," said Jake. "Let's have a cup of coffee. Besides there's something I need to talk to you about." The men walked back toward the house as the sun slowly started to peek above the trees.

Inside, the kitchen was big and cheerful. Esther and Nancy fried bacon and made biscuits, paying no attention to the two men who sipped their coffee contently.

"You know old man Pearson?" said Jake. "Word has it he's saying he's got the best hog meat around. Now from what I've seen of his pigs, they can't compare with ours. And these men here are the fastest cutters around. We'll beat everyone around here—easy."

"Oh," he paused. "I invited the Pearson Plantation over for the get-together afterwards. Do you mind?"

Henry looked up. "Jake, this is your house," he said. "Why should I mind?" He looked into Jake's eyes and was flattered that Jake would value his opinion.

"I asked," said Jake, "because everyone knows how Pearson is with his blacks. You know what happened to Tom Benton over there just last month? He treats his men like animals, and doesn't cater to the notion that a man treated fairly gives his best. Henry, I just wanted to show him that situations such as ours can work."

Henry studied the matter. Jake looked at him, hoping he'd agree. Finally Henry spoke up.

"Naw, it won't bother me none that Pearson's here. But Jake, you're such a trusting soul. Don't you know by now that a man such as Pearson, so set in his ways, ain't gonna change? He'll hate us 'til he dies, and worse, he hates you too. It seems to me, that you want him to approve of you more than my approval of him."

Jake sat back and sighed. "I know, you're right," he said. "I just wanted to try and change things. I know the other plantation owners don't approve of the way I run mine. But I gotta do what's best for me. I thought inviting Pearson would break the ice that's built up between the other owners and me."

"Then you did the right thing," said Henry. "If your heart says so, then it's right."

That said, both men set to a huge pile of hot biscuits, bacon and sorghum.

After breakfast Jake and a few of the hands headed to town for supplies. Henry went to the field to check on the men's progress, but stopped off at the barn first. He was met at the barn door by his son, Jim.

"Lookin for me?" Jim asked his Pa.

"Well, just lookin'," said Henry. Jim smiled at his Pa.

"Got news for you Pa," he said. "I got up a bit after Mr. Buchanan. I already fed the chickens, slopped the hogs, tended the horses and milked the cows. They're out to pasture now and I was just headin' for the field. I'm powerful hungry tho."

"Come on up to the house with me," said Henry.

The two walked toward the house, slowly, on purpose. The children had eaten and were commencing their work. It was times like this that Henry just didn't quite understand Jim. His middle child, so cold and hard, yet there was time like these. Time when there wasn't a better son to be found. Henry looked over at Esther.

"Is Millie up yet?" he asked.

"No," she answered. "But it's only a quarter past eight. She'll be up in time for the doings, bustling about in that big dress." They laughed, and Henry thought that this was the way family should be.

After Jim had eaten, Henry walked him out to the porch.

"Tell you what," he said. "That horse that's been givin' us so much trouble, why don't you take him out to the far right pasture and run him a spell?"

"You mean it, Pa?" said Jim, puzzled.

"Yep. Now mind you I said to run him, not push him." Henry put his arm around his son as they walked to the stables. I'll call you at hog killin' time," he yelled back as he headed out to the cotton fields.

And hog killin' it was. Everybody pitched in, running and yelping after them pigs like crazy. The squeals were deafening as the men wallowed in the mud, wrestling them. After they were killed, they were taken to an open area where hot water sat in big pots, bubbling. Here they were scalded to remove the hair. After a thorough scalding, they were hung on strong racks where they were split open, gutted, and left to hang so all the blood could drain out. This done, the men went to clean the mud and blood off themselves, for their job was not yet finished.

Jake, Millie, Henry and Esther sat in the yard, fanning and drinkin lemonade.

"Did you see that?" said Jake. "Did you see how fast that went?" Why, I bet we beat those other plantations, hands down!"

"You know it!" said Henry.

"But Miss Millie, you're looking a mite faint!" Millie was sitting stiffly in her chair. She fanned herself quickly, taking deep breaths.

"I guess all the to-do kinda makes me a bit queasy. Maybe I ought to go lie down."

"Maybe you ought to," said Jake, half laughing.

"You know," he said, "that woman gets sick every year when the hogs get killed. She should be like you, Esther—strong." Esther smiled, but she had to admit to herself that the whole thing was a bit upsetting.

Just then a wagon pulled up. Mr. Pearson got out, fat and important, strutting like he just won a sweepstakes.

"Your pigs still draining?" he asked Jake. Why, we've been through for an hour or so. Yep, I suppose we won, no holds barred. Oh, I just stopped by to tell you that me and the misses can't make your doings this evening. But I'll let some of my boys come on by later. Might let some of the women, too. I told ya if you'd put the whip to some of `um, they might of tried a little harder."

This said, he climbed back onto his wagon, heading home. As the men returned from their clean-up, Jake called them over.

"No need to rush," he said, Pearson just left and they're all done over there. Guess he beat us this year."

Henry spoke up. "Guess they did," he said. "But that don't matter none. Us here at the Buchanan Plantation ain't got nothing to prove to nobody. We've still got the best men, ain't we? Besides the old fool probably had them hogs killed yesterday. Well, come on now, lets get this done. There's a lot of doings on this evenin'."

And the men set to work. The hogs were all drained, so they separated the livers and the kidneys. They took out the intestines for chitterlings and the stomachs for tripe. The tongues were cut out for boiling and the sides cut for ham and chops. When almost every usable part was cut, Jake came over to distribute it. On the other plantations the men got only the intestines or tongue or kidneys. But Jake made sure that big ham portions went to all. The men gathered up their game and headed for their cabins. It was time for the women to prepare some of the hog meat. The other would be salted and stored for the winter months.

The air was light. The men lolled some-what, while the women prepared ham hocks, chitterlings, green beans, and sweet breads. The time went quick and soon buggies pulled up to the Buchanan Plantation. Men brought their guitars and harmonicas, singin' spiritual hymns and jumpy tunes that made everyone dance. Henry sat by Esther. He had long since given up dancin', and enjoyed just listenin' these days. Jake plunked his guitar, in time, remembering what a hard time Henry had teachin' him the chords. Millie had come out with the first twangs of the music to show off her pink dress. She milled about like a small bird, getting recipes and gossip, then runnin' back to Esther with it all.

"She is havin' a good time. Nobody could accuse her of being shy or frail tonight." Esther took Henry's arm, and looked him in the eyes. Then she whispered, "Besides, who could miss her in that bright pink dress?" He just smiled.

Henry looked at Jake, contentedly plucking his guitar and singing, making up the words he didn't know. He watched Millie innocently sharing secrets with Esther. He looked out at his children, dancin', singing, and havin' a ball. He wondered when they'd got so big. But what with running on the *River Boat*, he'd missed so much of their growing.

"This is how it should be," he thought. "Life was meant to live." Just then his son Jim walked up.

"Pa," he said, "You see that girl and that woman over there by the barn?" Henry focused his eyes.

"Yep," he said.

"Well, they're white Pa. Why does that woman let her daughter dance with black men?"

"True, the mother's white. She fell in love and married a young mulatto some time back. He was white enough to pass, but he didn't—or should I say wouldn't. Anyhow, she was totally pushed out from the whites after marrying him. Then after he died, and she'd had the girl, there wasn't nothing for her to do but work different places with the girl. Yeah, son, she may look white, but my guess is, she's black. Her name is Lula," Henry explained.

Jim looked at the girl. She was almost white, with hazel blue eyes and long brown hair. She sat demurely by her mother, getting up only when asked to dance. Looking up, she noticed Jim looking at her. Nervously she dropped her eyes, focusing on her hands in her lap.

"I figured she had a bit too much rhythm for white," laughed Jim. Then his eyes got serious. "She's the most beautiful girl I've ever seen!"

Henry watched his son. "Dear God," he thought. "He's become a man. My boy's become a man."

And so passed the years on the plantation. Jake tried to keep things as pleasant as possible, but there was lots of outside interference; yet he ran his plantation as he saw fit, and it prospered. Many times through adversity, it prospered. When hooded cowards burned a cross on his land, he and the men just doused the flames. When they burned his crops, they were replanted. When they burned his barn, it was rebuilt and they just couldn't understand how Jake, a white man, could stand it. Then finally the horror stopped. Seems it stopped with old man Pearson's death. Word had it he died when his horses stampeded and over-turned his buggy. Rumor had it, a spike went clear through him. But those at the Buchanan Plantation told a different story of his death—especially Jim.

Henry and Esther's children had all grown to adulthood, and some had taken mates. Those who wished to stay had small homes on the land. Jim courted and married Lula and they lived out back of the plantation. Still, his restlessness continued. Even as the children came, it continued. He often went to town, meeting with small groups of men—angry men who wanted change. He would talk to them, far into the night, then come home angry at the woman whose color stood for all he hated so. There were days when Lula bent beside the ashes in the fireplace, smearing them on her fair skin, in desperation. There were days she raised her beautiful face to the hot sun, hoping it would bake her, color her, and make her the black woman that Jim could adore. There were rumors of another woman, a black woman named Carrie, but Lula ignored this talk. She knew Jim loved her, and she despised those who said she wasn't good enough. Why, her and Jim had two fine sons, Roosevelt and Wendell. Their skin was as white as hers. And even if Jim treated them with indifference, they were the only joy in Lula's life.

Millie came down with a cancer in the winter and died two weeks after Thanksgiving. Esther tended her as best she could, but Millie always was sickly and unable to do much.

As they stood at her grave, in the cemetery out back of the big house, Esther thought of how years before she had likened Millie to a bird, flitting about in her pink dress. She put her arms around Nancy, who cried silently. Henry steadied Jake, who seemed to reel from grief. He held him and spoke soothing words that meant nothing to Jake at this time. Finally, he whispered to Esther and his family to go to the house. And they walked away, silently, leaving Jake to his good-byes.

Jake wasn't much good after that. He demanded more and more of Henry's time, wantin' to sit and drink lemonade and talk—talk about Millie, the *River Boat*, and about hog killin'. Henry obliged him, for they were both too old now to do much else. They sat and rocked and laughed at how white their hair was, how feeble their minds were, but they still had their memories. They still had yesterday, even though tomorrow came faster than they realized; then spring, then summer.

One summer night Lula sat looking out the window of their cabin, listening to the night rain fall steadily on the roof. On and on it came, beating rhythms like a drum, bending the willow trees against their will. She thought of her mother—hated and tormented for loving a man of the wrong color. She thought of herself, tormented for being the wrong color. She thought of her children. Then she heard the buggy wheel turn into the yard. She watched as Jim pulled up sitting along side a black woman, a woman as dark as the night. She covered up her children and lay on the soft bunk. Tears filled her eyes. Hate filled her heart, but not for Jim. For herself. She looked at her hands, visible even in darkness. She waited.

Jim opened the door and came in, filling the room with smells of liquor and tobacco. He stumbled against the table and sat heavily in a straight wooden chair, looking at the rain. The buggy pulled away and Lula sat up, wondering what to say.

Jim spoke up. "Did you hear about them lynching Jed Matthews this evenin'? Did ya hear they hung him, then burned him?"

Jim held his head in his hands as Lula came to his side. She knew Jim and Jed had long been friends.

"No, I hadn't heard," she whispered, putting her arms around her husband. Jim jumped straight up like her touch stung him. He faced Lula, his eyes flaring.

"Your people!" he yelled. "Probably one of your own kin tied the knot!"

Lula covered her mouth, backing up with Jim in pursuit. The blows came again and again. Jim grabbed her hair, flinging her across the room into the children's bed. Lula lay there praying as Jim stood over her, shouting, flinging his arms. She glanced at the bed, only to find Roosevelt looking at his father in rage.

Jumping up, Roosevelt screamed, "Just go away. Don't hit my mother!" His tiny fists hit at his father's legs. Jim grabbed the boy, holding him high, looking him in the eyes, then flung him across the room and stormed out into the night and the rain. Lula gathered Wendell and Roosevelt to her, laying still, willing her heart not to beat so, lest he hear her and return. She listened as the rain, which had once sounded melodies, now beat mercilessly into the ground. She listened to Jim's raging, and the machine spun around and around with Jim at the controls. Then she heard the scream—the piercing scream that seemed to stop the night—then quiet and stillness.

Putting the children back on the bed, she raced for the door in time to see Jake Buchanan bending over a still form.

"Run to the house!" Jake yelled at her. "Get Henry and Esther!"

Although in pain, Lula ran across the yard, but was met halfway by Esther and Henry. They, too, had heard the screams.

"Child, what happened to you?" said Henry, but he knew all too well.

"Esther, take her up to the house and tend to her," he said. "I'm going to Jim."

Henry bent down by his son, who laid still on the wet ground.

"Seems he got tangled up in this here thrasher," said Jake. "We gotta get him to a doctor, quick, or he'll bleed to death."

Henry closed his eyes, and nodded. "Well, we'd better take him to Doc Fullum's up the way. Will Fullum and his wife, Corrine, will fix him up." Jake knew this was so.

"I'll load him up in the wagon," Henry said.

"Now you hurry inside, and put on some shoes and a shirt." Jake looked down. In the rush, he had run out of the house with just his pants on. He hurried to the house as Henry pulled his boy onto the wagon. Sitting on top he looked at Jim, wondering if this rage would ever stop. Jake took the reins and sped down the bend to Doc Fullum's. Henry moved to the back of the wagon, cradling Jim, covering him with a blanket. Doc Fullum told them that Jim was mangled pretty bad, but his arm was the worst. It would have to come off, or he'd die. He advised them to let Jim rest there a day or two after the amputation. Henry leaned heavily against the wall and nodded at Jake. Jake lowered his eyes and reached for his pipe, and Henry reached for the matches.

Time passed. Jake was sickly most of the time, his cough bad, his body frail. Esther again set to task—with the help of Nancy tending to him— keeping him comfortable.

Jim and Lula had two more children, Essie and Anna. His accident hadn't changed him—only made him worse. She'd watch him as he rubbed the wooden arm with the hook on the end. She knew he blamed her, and each time there was a lynching, a killing, she'd feel his wrath, his hook.

Henry grew old gracefully and watched over all as he sat beside Jake, often spinning tales that neither had ever lived. His other son, Will, had come back to live and Henry was grateful for that. Will could always take the edge off of Jim, chastising him often for his treatment of Lula. It took some of the pressure off of Henry.

That Friday Jake didn't come down for breakfast. Esther told Henry that Jake had had a bad night and preferred to eat in his room. Henry picked up his coffee cup and went upstairs. He pulled up a chair and looked at Jake, who seemed pale, but perked at the site of him.

"Thought I'd come up," he said. "Let's sit and talk a spell." And the old men talked. They talked of yesterday, for that was all that was left now. They sat all afternoon, laughing, drumming up the *River Boat*. They talked of Millie, Esther and the children. Henry ate lunch, then dinner with Jake, who brought up the broom jumping, the tiny bird, and even Millie's pink dress. He had so much to say.

Esther sat down stairs in the kitchen—quiet—sewing tiny dresses for her grandchildren, Essie and Anna. She thought of the two babies who were so different from the boys. Essie, impish and mischievous. Anna, tiny and almost sad. She couldn't understand how, even though she was a baby, Anna seemed to be so lonely. Henry came to the kitchen.

"Esther, wanna fix us up some lemonade?" he asked. "Jake has a hankering for lemonade."

Esther looked into her husband's eyes. They were so drawn and sad. She wanted to say something, anything, but some things are better left unsaid. Nancy came and helped her make the lemonade. Both women worked in silence. Handing the tray to Henry, they watched as he walked slowly up the stairs to his friend. Esther hugged Nancy, but no words were spoken.

Henry poured the lemonade, handed a glass to Jake, and sat down slowly in the old rocker as Jake pulled the covers around his neck.

"Getting kinda chilly out, ain't it?" he asked.

Henry looked out the window. The sun was still up, it was still warm.

"Yep, it's getting chilly out," he said.

Jake took a few sips of his lemonade, then laughed.

"You think Will ever forgave us for gettin' him beat about those mince pies?" he asked.

Henry smiled. "Oh, he forgave us," he said. "He forgave us."

Jake leaned back and reached for his pipe and an envelope. Henry lit the pipe, leaning forward, looking into Jake's eyes through the flames. Jake handed Henry the envelope and settled back on the pillow. He cleared his throat and closed his eyes, as if the effort were too much. Finally he spoke.

"If something should ever happen to me, Henry, say maybe ten, fifteen years from now, open this letter. Not before, but only when I'm gone."

Henry shivered. Jake's words cut right through him. He had the same feeling when waitin' for Jake by the fence, as a boy, or when Jake had told him about the *River Boat*. Shaking all this aside, he took Jake's hand.

"We've got a lot of time to think such things," he said.

"Lots of time. Besides, tomorrow's Hog Killin' Day." Jake smiled.

"Yep, and we'll beat 'um all," he said. Jake's voice was low and in a whisper. "Henry, you're just like a brother to me. My family, my friend, my brother. Would you turn on the light now? It's so dark in here."

Henry sat still. The sun was just going over the horizon. Gently he reached and covered Jake up, whispering, "just like a brother," as he gently took the pipe from his hand. And all night he sat there—slowly rocking, and softly crying—for Jake was quiet now, the night had come.

The next day Henry buried Jake out back next to Millie. It was a gathering of plantations as everyone gathered to pray and say good-bye. They wept, then left Henry for his moment. Henry sat all day and far into the night in the damp grass beside the grave. The night winds came, yet he stared into the night, remembering things that he'd long since forgotten. He wondered when they'd grown so old. Getting up, he started back to the house, walking slowly, shaking his head, as if to wake up from a bad dream.

Inside the house Esther and the family sat motionless at the huge dinner table that once fed them all. No one sat at the head. Lula and Nancy prepared hot tea and warm milk for Essie and Anna. Roosevelt and Wendell sat by the mantel whittling whistle sticks quietly. Jim, Will and Mayo decided to go out back to check the stables. Esther touched her husband's hand, but said no words. She dabbed at her eyes with a hankie, looking at the pretty doilies that Millie had once made. Henry stared down at his cup of tea, swallowing slowly. Blowing his nose, he commented that the rag weed must of got to him.

With the house and stables all checked, Jim and Will came back to the house. Will sat beside Esther, while Jim went into the kitchen. Reaching for a cup, Lula poured him a cup of tea. Jim looked in her eyes. They were red from crying. Putting his arms around her, he held her to him. "Mr. Buchanan was the first person to ever show me kindness," she said softly, as Jim gently stroked her hair. Then gathering up their children, they went to their small house, with Jim carrying Anna close to him. Everyone then retired to their separate quarters.

Henry walked around the huge house putting out all the lanterns. His heart was leaden, and he was somehow afraid. He knew this was one time Jake couldn't stand by his side. He climbed the stairs, pausing at Jake's door. Pushing it open, he went inside, stopping at the window, looking towards the cemetery, way over the fields. The room smelt of tobacco and of Jake. He looked at the small table beside the bed. "Jake's pipe," he thought as he tapped out the tobacco and put it in his pocket. Sighing, he went out the door and down the hall to his room.

Esther was lying quiet, still on her side. "She must be asleep," Henry thought. "It's been a long day for her too." Esther lie staring at the wall. She knew there were times when men needed to be left alone.

As Henry sat on the edge of the bed to undress, the envelope fell out of his shirt pocket. "Jake's letter," he thought, pulling a chair over to the window. Then lighting a lantern, he sat down, fumbling with the letter's seal.

Dear Henry,
            By the time you read this, I'll be somewhere else, waitin' for you. We'll see each other again. I've thought this decision out carefully, and you being the man you are, I know you'll abide by it. Millie agreed.
            Before I took sick, I took it upon myself to go to town and have a few things changed. Henry, the whole plantation is yours, deed and all. I had everything changed over to your name. Except the deed reads, Henry Buchanan. See, I changed your name, too. You're now Henry Buchanan.
            You're like a brother to me, Henry, and I'll rest in peace, knowing we share everything. My home is yours— for you, Esther and the families to live in forever. I could never let you down, Henry, and this way we'll still be together. There are lots of memories in this house. And when you come to meet me, divide the plantation among your own, as you see fit. It's all been settled in town.
            It's a long road from the little bird, to the River Boat, to here, and I know you'll miss me. But there ain't two men on this earth that has more memories than we have. Just think of them, and you'll smile. For we grew old together.
            Have a good life, Henry Buchanan, and carry my name with pride. For it's with pride that I give it to you.

Your Friend , far past this day,
Jake

    Henry slowly folded the letter, deeds and other papers. He lay down, his hands behind his head, staring at the ceiling.   He smiled. "Jake never let me down," he thought. "He never let me down."

Things went well on the plantation. The men responded well to Henry, respecting his wishes. Jim took over as supervisor, running things with a firm hand. He seemed somewhat settled, staying home more, drinking less. His manner with Lula changed some and she was happy. The children were doing well, and Anna—the baby, who was generally quite sickly—began to flourish. Lula worried about her because she was so tiny. Jim noticed too, and paid special attention to Anna. The others he tolerated, but Anna was special to him. He would hold the tiny baby for hours, talking to her, laughing at her, laughing at her red freckles. It was rare to see Jim laugh so.

A few months on, Esther took ill. She felt tired. She didn't seem to get around quite like she used to. Henry looked at her across the dinner table. Her eyes were so drawn as she picked at her food.

"You children clear up dinner," Henry said. "Ma's gonna go up and lay down." Esther told all good night, holding Anna close to her.

"You're special, Anna," she whispered in the baby's ear, and handed her back to Lula to nurse. Then, leaning slightly on Henry, she climbed the stairs to their room.

He put his wife to bed and headed downstairs and out to the back gate. Sitting beside the old oak, he sobbed. He pictured Esther, young, beautiful, standing at the door of their small house, waiting for him to return from the *River Boat*. His heart ached, thinking how she never did for herself, but took care of all the others, even staying up three nights with Anna's whooping cough. He thought of the small old woman who lay in the bed, hair gray and eyes tired. His heart pounded as if it would beat out of his chest, but how could it? For surely it was broken.

"Dear Jesus!" he cried into the night. "Dear Jesus, give me the strength I need now!" And he walked back to the house, to the room, and lay beside his wife.

Esther raised her head a little and lay on Henry's shoulder.

"I'm tired Henry," she said softly. "I'm so tired." Then Henry kissed his wife's brow whispering, "Just sleep Es," and she slept—a sleep Henry knew from which she'd never awaken.

After Esther's burial, there wasn't much left for Henry. He walked around the land talking to himself a lot, or just sat on the porch drinkin' lemonade. He went to the grave site and sat in silent prayer or just stared into the sky, as the birds flew. He thought of all that had been, as he rocked alone in his chair—a lonely old man with his memories.

It was gray and cool on this day in autumn as Henry walked the path to Jim's house. He wrapped his worn sweater tighter about him, asking Lula if she had any seltzer handy. His insides needed a little calming, and he figured it must have been those hog maws he ate at noon.

Lula fixed the seltzer, gave it to Henry, then went to the stables to find Jim. She found him tending a new colt.

"You better come on up to the house," she told him. "Your Pa's lookin' a mite bad." Jim smoothed the pony's coat and headed for the house with Lula.

Inside, Henry leaned back in a straight wooden chair as Lula wet a rag with cold water to put on his head.

"Better lay down on this cot over here Papa," she said gently to the old man who was the only father she'd ever known. Henry lay down and Jim covered him with a blanket. Pulling up the wooden chair, he sat beside his father, then sent Lula up to the big house to get his brother Will. He held his father's hand and prayed softly.

Lula headed down the path, but stopped just short of the big house. Out front were three or four wagons with angry whites piling out, screaming, yellin', and shouldering their guns. She stood behind a large tree watching in terror, and prayin' her two boys wouldn't run along the path.

The men's yells brought Will out of the house. His eyes darted from one to the other as they shouted their obscenities. Clearing his throat, he stared at the first of them directly in the eyes.

"This is our land," he said sternly, "willed to us after Jake Buchanan died. You're trespassin' on our land."

The crowd grew still. Will swallowed hard, but stood his ground. Then, through the silence, a single shot, and he fell lifeless to the porch steps.

The shot startled Jim, who nearly jumped from his chair. Stumbling, he raced for the door, then down toward the house. Lula met him, her eyes wide, her face pale.

"Get the children and stay in the house!" he yelled to her as he ran on. A tall fat man with a cigar stopped him.

"Want something, boy?" he snarled. "You got some business here?"

Jim glared at the man. He watched as the others went in and out of his house, ransacking it, tearing up papers, drinking the liquor. He watched as they walked over his brother Will's body as if it were dirt. He blinked his eyes, hoping this nightmare would end.

"I asked you a question!" yelled the man.

Jim's head snapped. His eyes flared.

"This is my house!" he screamed. "That's my business here! And that's my brother, there. Dear God, you've killed my brother!"

Jim headed for Will, who still lay on the steps.

"Stop right where you are!" the man yelled, but Jim kept right on walking. He cradled Will's head in his arms, wiping the blood with his shirt. Two men came out on the porch as the first man cocked his gun at Jim's head.

"Hold on there now," one of them said.

Jim looked up, recognizing him to be old man Pearson's son. "That there's Jim McBride. He's all right. Why, I've known him since we were boys." The man put down his gun. "Besides I got what we came for. I found the deed."

Jim tensed with rage. He picked up his brother, and headed for his house. The walk seemed endless. His heart beat wildly as rage filled him. He was aware that three men followed him, but he didn't care. He kept walking.

Laying his brother on the porch, he went inside his small house, the men close behind him. Lula and the children huddled in a corner. Not even the baby whimpered. They looked around the house as Jim bent over his father, still lying on the cot.

"Wake him up!" yelled one of the men. "We've got to start assigning chores, gotta get this place run the way it should be. The old man oughta be good for something!"

Jim took his father's hand and squeezed it tight. Standing up to face the men, he spoke softly.

"He's gone," he said. "My father's dead."

Then Pearson's son spoke up. "Well, have some of them hands build a couple of caskets for your Pa and your brother. I want them buried today. I sure don't need no blacks just laying around. Put 'um right out back in the yard. That should do!" Then they left, slamming the door behind them.

Jim sat down heavily in the wooden chair. He looked at his father's face, which was smooth and peaceful.

"Lula," he whispered. "Get some of the hands to build a couple of caskets. Tell 'um to make 'um strong and big."

Lula did as she was told. Jim looked down at his father, his anger subsiding, and cried. He cried for all that had been and for all he should have done. He cried openly, unashamed, and not caring that his children watched in silence. Then he went outside to make the markers for their final resting place. He dug two plots right out in back of the house, then went to talk to some of the hands. Pulling a few aside, he instructed them to wait 'til dark, then go out back and fill up the holes he had dug. They agreed, never asking any questions.

When night fell, Jim hitched the horses to the wagon. Putting the casket and markers inside, he headed across the field to Buchanan Cemetery. He dug two graves and laid his brother and his father to rest beside their loved ones. Jim sat down in the grass, thinking how glad he was that they were all at peace, and all together again.

He wiped away tears as he whispered, "Papa, I tried to change. I really tried, but they won't let you. They only want to make you less of a man. Daddy, from now on things'll be done as I gotta do 'um. Just please believe that I tried." Climbing back on the wagon, he started for the house, knowing that it was no longer home. He felt again that he was nothing, and again the rage that he thought had subsided wailed within. He looked back at his father's marker. It read: *Rest in Peace, Henry Buchanan.*

BOTH SIDES OF THE FENCE

And so were the lives of Jim and Lula in the old shack out back of the plantation. From all that had been, there was nothing, not even hope.

Many a night Jim would stand by the north orchard watching the flickering lights of Buchanan Plantation, the sounds of music and revelry cutting the air, and his heart raged. He hated the clear people inside and swore their blood was of water from a tainted stream. He hated the fact that they ignored him, on a land that was rightfully his. He hated the smell of their clear cooking in the air, and wondered what beat in their chests that make them so deceiving. For if everyone is God's creation, where did they come from? And Jake Buchanan, why was he so different?

All Jim had were his thoughts now, for they had long since taken all his dreams. He thought way back to the stories his father told of being sold in front of the store, and he knew that things were not much better now. He thought of his mother Esther and her warmth, and longed to see her, knowing she lie still, at peace, in the cemetery out back. He thought of Jake, so kind, and even Millie, who although strange, couldn't harm a fly. And he leaned against the apple tree, sighing in the relief that they'd never see the way things had become. The doors to the large house opened and a small group spilled outside—laughing and talking like the world was theirs. They climbed into their wagons, their faces stark and white against the night, and rode right past him, never noticing that he was there, with his heart, and his bottle in his hands. And his resentment grew like the weeds around the small shack.

Lula managed as best she could, for she had long since learned to make do. She'd grown strong from years of resentment and scorn that went way back—for it wasn't just starting now. Her mother, who dared to be different, had taught her that this was her lot, and she'd learned early that she'd never be accepted by either side.

Sometimes she smiled when she thought of when she and Jim were first married. He'd thought she was so beautiful, but in her mind, she felt she could never compare with the bronzed dark beauties around. So she would sit by the fireplace and put soot on her face to darken it and greet Jim when he came in from the fields. How he would laugh. Yes, he used to actually laugh and spin her around, her long hair hitting his face. Now she was careful to keep it tightly pinned up, for she knew her skin, her eyes, her hair, exemplified everything that he despised. Now they served only as a constant reminder. And she was always reminded. She felt the brunt of all of Jim's pain. In his drunken tirades, she would sit quietly, listening to his plans for those who had betrayed him, and often her mind drifted to taking her children and running. But where? Where could she go? She knew no one would take her in, much less four pale children that looked like her. The ranting usually led to beatings and all she felt was relief when he left to spend time with Carrie, who he said, understood. Still, she loved him and understood far more than he realized. For she, too, was caught in the middle.

The children were coming along fine, but Anna was still so tiny. Her hazel eyes were sad, and always far away. Maybe she, too, realized her lot in life. Jim wasn't home too much, as he divided his time between there and Carrie's. Carrie had four children by him too and he flaunted them openly. They were dark like him and Carrie, and he was proud. He mostly ignored his children by Lula, except for Anna. He loved Anna. She was his youngest, and often he'd set aside a special piece of sugar cane just for her. Doc and Roosevelt feared him, Essie defied him, but Anna looked him right in the eye. Many times he said that she was far too wise to be a mere baby. He loved her, and didn't try to hide it.

Sometimes he would hoist her onto his shoulders and take her out back to his still to watch him make his whiskey. Although she was barely three, he would tell her the stories of the plantation, and how he lost his arm. He'd let her touch his hook that served as a hand and play in the barley as he filled the big jugs. Once, as he was killin' a chicken, it jumped off the block with its head cut off and chased Anna. Jim laughed and laughed as her little legs ran around and around the yard, the headless chicken in hot pursuit. Lula and the other children ran to the yard, laughing wildly at the little girl who never wanted to be a spectacle. Anna stopped running. She turned around, the chicken crashing into her, and they both dropped limp, to the ground.

Then, Anna dragged the chicken over to Jim and said, "Here Daddy." Jim then cradled her in his arms. Yes, there were times, but they were few and far between. For Jim was always sure not to be too happy, lest he forget.

Sometimes when Jim would either be on a whiskey run or visiting with Carrie, Essie and Anna would go with their mother to the river to wash clothes. These times Lula would let her hair down and sing, a faint song only barely remembered.

She would tell the girls of beaus and barn dances and how Jim had won her heart. She'd tell them of her mother who'd died so young, and of the big house up the hill. She assured them that it was theirs and tried to explain why their father was so angry, and the young girls listened. Especially Anna. For her small mind knew there had to be a reason for so much pain.

Doc and Roosevelt kept mostly to themselves. They were handsome boys, good boys, who worked hard and never talked back. They had learned early to stay clear of their father, who assumed any show of affection would make them weak. They played their own games, and dreamed of being rich farmers, detesting his treatment of their mother, yet loving him just the same.

Essie fought him tooth and nail. Her temper was fiery and she was walloped practically every day, which only served to make her more defiant. She was pretty and she knew it, priding herself on her perfect features. Four years older than Anna, she was fiercely protective of her, often telling her they'd be together forever.

Nights in the small house were quiet when Jim was gone. When he was home, he spent most of his time out back with his still, or drinking with some of the other men. The smell of *rotgut* was overwhelming at times, but Lula didn't mind. It kept him away from her and gave her more time with her children. After walking them down the way to the outhouse, she would pull them to her—for in the small room they would laugh and talk, and once in a while, when he was in a rare mood, Jim would watch them. He always held Anna, looking in her somber eyes and rocking her in the wooden chair that was his father's.

The other nights Lula would sit alone in the rocking chair, humming her faint song, and staring in the direction of the house where Jim spent so much of his time.

Jim's sister, Nancy, lived down the way and visited Lula often. She loved the children, and enjoyed being with them, as she was barren and never married. Sometimes she would bring over pie, or a batch of hot cinnamon sticks, or just some chicory for coffee, but her visits were welcomed—even by Jim. For these were the times that they would sit and talk of yesterday—of roasts and music and of hog killin' day, of Ma and Pa, and all that was. Anna always listened, her small mind absorbed with the chatter of those who knew. Even while the other children ran out to play, Anna listened, sitting snugly at her mother's feet.

Sometimes Nancy would take the children to her house for a few days, and how they loved it. Her house was larger and neater than Jim's, and there were flowers along the rickety broom fence. Essie and the boys delighted in tearing through the yard chasing the chickens or climbing trees. Anna would sit by the fence, making small bouquets with the daisies for her sun bleached auburn hair. Aunt Nancy would slip her an extra cinnamon stick sometimes, and Anna would lean against the fence post, thinking child's thoughts, or playing games with the beetles. Aunt Nancy would stroke Anna's soft hair and wonder why so young a child's eyes could be so sad and far away.

One particularly hot day, Nancy walked the children home after a short visit. Her graying hair was streaked with sweat, and her heart was sad, for she had received a telegram about her and Jim's sister, Fanny. It seems she had caught a cancer, and had passed on a few days ago. Nancy walked slowly with Anna clinging to her hand. Tears stung her eyes, but she was careful to shield them from the children as they mingled with moisture from her brow. Fanny was the baby, and she pictured her bustling about the kitchen on Buchanan Plantation, or making fun of Miss Millie, and remembered how sad she felt when Fanny had left to go up North to marry Paul Reed, but Fanny had done fine. Paul had a small blacksmith shop and they made ends meet, times as they were. They had kept in touch, but

Fanny's last letter was vague. She'd told Nancy she was sick, but not how sick. She'd said there was no need to come. Now she was gone, and as Nancy walked the path to the house, she felt tired—suddenly so tired.

Jim took Fanny's death quietly and went out back to his still. With her gone, there was just him, Mayo and Nancy left to the immediate family. He sat down heavily, the smell of liquor encasing him. Opening a new jug, he turned it up. Funny how he seemed to think that drinking would make it better, while the others in the house knew better.

Lula sat by Nancy on the tattered couch listening patiently. She smiled at stories about chitlins and pink petticoats. It seemed their life had been so much better than her own had. An only child, Lula was often scorned, and scuttled with her mother from place to place. She was the girl that neither side accepted, and she never had learning like Jim and Nancy. Blinking back to reality, she was met by Anna's solemn eyes, and she knew what she must do. Then taking Nancy's hands, she spoke slowly, softly.

"Would you teach my children to read?" she asked. "Can you teach them about books and lands and math?" And Nancy smiled—a wide smile with gleaming teeth. And she admitted to Lula that she'd been teachin' them a little all along.

So Nancy took to task. Every day at noon the children would run down the way to her house, and she was surprised at how fast they learned. Especially Anna. She was so young, yet her memory and learning were amazing, and even after the other children tired, she would linger, to be read another story. When Nancy took the children home, they would tell their mother all that they'd learned that day.

One day as Nancy walked the children home from a Bible lesson, they were met by screams from within the house. Painful screams and broken glass pierced the early evening, as Nancy, telling the children to wait, raced up the walk. Inside the darkening house, the streak of Jim's silver hooked hand lashed the air. Lula laid at his feet, her lovely face red, swollen and bloody. All her fight was gone as she took the blows as well as any man. Nancy squinted, then reached in her petticoat and pulled out her gun, spinning Jim around to face her.

"Hit her again and you're dead," she yelled, pushing him into the wall, her eyes as blazen and dark as his. Cursing and blinking, he looked hard at his sister, but he also knew her. And he knew that she would kill him. He staggered out the door, past his children, and made his way to Carrie's. The children watched in silence, as their father wavered past them, never looking down. Doc and Roosevelt stepped aside feeling helpless and angry as Essie smiled, for she loved to see her father defeated.

Anna went inside and watched as Nancy washed Lula's wounds. She dabbed water on her mother's face and cried. She hated the things he did to her mother, yet she pitied him too. She couldn't understand why he was so angry every day. What was it, inside, that tormented him so?

And Lula wept openly. For herself, her children and for Jim. Holding Nancy's hands to her face, she knew what she must do.

"Nancy," she started slowly, her voice barely a whisper, "please take my children from all this. Promise me you'll take them!" Nancy held her, as a mother holds a small child. She held her.

"Don't you worry none," she whispered. "We'll take care of everything tomorrow." But Lula knew for her there was no tomorrow. Just living today was hard enough. She knew there was no place to go, no where to turn, for she was hated on both sides of the fence.

Morning peaked and the house was unusually quiet. The children busied themselves while Nancy tended to Lula. Jim stayed away for a few days, probably figuring it would all be okay when he came home.

At Carrie's, Jim sat sullenly looking at the children and the mess he had created. Carrie was quiet, for she knew that she fared no better than Lula with Jim, and she knew when to be silent.

A squealing buggy pulled up outside and Jim watched Ben Tomkins pull up. The back loaded with moonshine.

"I'm almost filled up," he yelled as he walked in, his rolled cigarette hanging from his mouth. "I went by your place but when I didn't see your buggy, I naturally came here," he trailed off. "When will your load be ready for town?"

"Soon as I get up to the house," Jim responded as the two men walked outside.

"I'll meet you by the creek tonight. There's a bit more barley I need to add to mine."

Pulling off in his wagon, Jim watched as his small house came into view. He looked at the splintered wood and weak stilts that held it high off the ground. He looked at the weeds that seemed to have a mind of their own. And he looked at the small figure that played and sang under the house with doodle-bugs.

Harnessing the horses, he listened to the sweet song that small Anna sang with her tiny friends.

"Back, back, doodle, back, back," Anna sang as the bugs squirmed in the dirt, making small poofs.

Then Jim reached under the porch to scoop up the child that could warm his heart so. And she looked in his eyes and touched his face as he walked up the stairs to the house.

Inside Lula stood by the iron stove cooking vegetables. She never turned as she reached for the bacon fat to season the batch. Staring blankly through swollen eyes, she watched as Jim carried Anna out back to his still. And Lula wondered how, why had things gone so wrong? Were the people of whom she was so much a part really to blame? Getting bowls from the counter she filled them, putting them on the small table, careful to save a large portion for Jim. Calling Essie, she asked her to get the boys, their father, and Anna.

At the table the children ate with zeal while Lula stared quietly at her bowl. Jim ate quickly, never looking at Lula. They rarely looked at each other anymore. Scooting his chair back, he headed out back to his still. He figured he could think of other things later.

Jim headed for the creek to meet Ben about ten. Before he got full there, Ben met him, running up to his wagon, puffing.

"They got me Jim," Ben said, his eyes wide, nose flaring. "The Revenuers got my whole load. I got away this time, but I tell you, it's too dangerous to make a haul tonight."

Jim steadied his horses, pulling sharply on the reins. Then turning them around, he headed back to the house, his mind full of his stash. He knew he had to sell it. There was no money. Pulling up sharply, he raced into the house, yelling for Lula and the children to get up.

"You gotta make this run with me," he told them as they scrambled into clothes for the ride. "They're less likely to stop a family than a man riding alone. Get in the wagon."

They followed him out to the wagon with tired eyes and jittery nerves—Jim securing Anna between him and Lula. The other children sat in the back with the brew, as Jim raced to town, his hook clutching the reins tightly. The winds rushed through Lula's hair, and it fell lifeless at her shoulders, unable to maintain its neatness. It felt good to let it blow even though her heart was gripping with fear for her children. Anna held fiercely to her seat, the bumps rocking her from side to side as she watched her father and then her mother. Then Jim noticed a flicker up ahead. A lantern was a ways up the path and he knew what that meant. Slowing his pace, he brought his horses to a trot, as the lantern's glare grew as large as Anna's eyes. She was terrified but she didn't know of what, and the tears came—she couldn't stop them. They just came, against the harsh protests of her father who demanded that she stop. Finally reaching in his pocket, Jim drew a small gun, pointed it at Anna, and said, "Shut her up or I'll kill her!" Anna looked in his eyes. They were cold and deep, and Lula pulled the young girl to her, begging her to stop.

"Please," she begged, as the lantern was upon them. "Please think of the doodle-bugs and their song." And Anna stopped, sinking into her mother's softness as children do.

Jim gripped his gun as the men stopped the wagon. He knew they cared nothing that his family was with him, but if anything happened, he intended to take a few with him.

"What are you hauling?" one of the men drawled, as two others poked in the wagon.

"Children," snapped Jim. "Children!"

"Never felt no children like this," the man went on as he reached past Essie and grabbed a jug.

"Well, looka here," he sneered at the other men as he smashed the bottle to the ground. "Get down from the wagon! You know you folks with your moonshine are making it hard on us legit liquor sellers. Why, just this evening one of you tried to make a run, but we got the haul, and he ran. He thought he'd get away but we got him too. It was awful stupid of him to come back down this path."

Jim's mind raced. They'd killed Ben. If he'd gone on home instead of trying to warn him, he'd be safe. But they'd got him and Jim's insides raged. He hated them. He hated them with all that he was.

Climbing from the wagon, Jim stood close by the horses, careful to hold on to the reins. He watched as the men smashed his bounty and his money, in a rage that rivaled none. Anna's small eyes were wide. She couldn't understand such anger, such hate. Her mother and the other children were quiet as the melee went on, and when the men walked to the front of the wagon, all held their breath.

Then Jim, quick as lightning, reached in his coat for the gun. "Stop right there," he ordered, his mind racing through every cruel deed their kind had ever done. It was silent for what seemed like forever. Silent. Except for the men's labored pants that mingled with the dirt. Jim lowered the barrel, clickin' the level with a sound that pierced the night. His hand squeezed the trigger, and his heart was filled with deep, inner joy as sweat poured from his brow in unchecked patterns. Then Anna raced to the side of the wagon. Her tiny hands grabbed her father's arm, and the bullet, with deafening clarity, raced through the trees. And all were shocked in sudden reality as Jim leaped into the wagon, thrashing the horses into order. And off they raced, jostling the children from side to side, the wheels kicking dust on the trio that still lay face down in the dust.

Pulling the wagon out back of the house, Jim hurried Lula and the children inside. He tied the horses out back of the shed, and stood glaring into the night, his anger unsubsided, but now directed at all.

"Walk, Jim, walk. Don't go in the house," his mind kept saying, but his feet kept walking. Walking up the path, up the stairs, and into the room where Lula and the children sat huddled, knowing what was to come.

Jim reached for a bottle from the cabinet and sat facing them. He didn't bother to pour, he just drank it in massive gulps as he stared at Anna. Anna, the child that he loved so. Who'd have thought that she'd dash his one chance to get even.

"Bring her here!" Jim commanded Lula. "Bring Anna to me."

Lula got up slowly, holding Anna closely, and screamed her defiance. "No Jim," she answered. "No! I won't let you take your failure out on my children. See, I'm used to it. I don't care anymore. But not my babies. I won't let you hurt my babies."

"Fair enough," Jim replied, as he grabbed Lula's throat, landing a blow that sent her crumbling to the ground. And she looked at him with eyes devoid of fear or feeling. Essie grabbed Anna's hand and tried to shield her eyes. Doc and Roosevelt ran to their mother, jumping on their father's back, hitting him with fists that meant nothing. Jim shrugged them off, flinging them to the floor, as Lula screamed.

"Run. Run to Aunt Nancy's!" And they ran, pulling Anna along as she clung desperately to the doorway. She wanted to stay. She needed to stay, but Essie drug her down the path in a flight for life.

The children pounded on Aunt Nancy's door, but no one answered. It seems she was in the next county visiting her friends. The night grew chilly as the children huddled together under the bent oak out front of the house. Soon they dozed, except for Anna. Her small eyes peered into the night in hurt and anger. She knew something was different about this night.

In the morning she woke the other children, knowing they must go home to check on their mother. They found her still crumbled by the fireplace. Her eyes were glazed. They looked far away, only this time not quite so sad. She moved slightly, very slowly, but managed to prop herself against the hearth. She smiled at them, a mother's smile, as the boys tried to fix her something to eat. She smiled as Essie got a chair and gently helped her into it and she smiled as Anna got a warm rag and pulled up a crate to stand on. And as young Anna stood on the box, softly washing and untangling her mothers matted hair, she cried. She cried as she felt the knots, and holes, Jim's hook had left. She cried as the blood rushed from Lula's face with the water's touch. Lula held Anna to her. She stroked her auburn hair, and dried her eyes with a dress soaked in blood, and whispered the words of comfort that only a mother knows.

Doc and Roosevelt were outside picking collards when distant dust from out back signaled that their father was coming home. Racing in the house they told their mother she must leave, hide, and they would bring her the food and clothes she needed.

Lula staggered out the front door, pausing only long enough to look back at her children. Crossing the field slowly, she crouched behind the barren apple tree that had so often served as a haven. Peering out, she saw the wagon stop. She saw Jim, Carrie, and their children pile out, suitcases and bundles in tow. She saw her childrens' faces, pale as they faced quite the unknown. And she watched as Carrie looked around, gloating over what now was all hers. Then, with a heart that beat just barely, Lula headed back to her house and her children. With steps that pained with every movement, she walked with one goal in mind—her children.

Jim stood with Carrie on the porch, watching as Lula made her painful trek. She reached the edge of the lane and spoke with forced breaths that told all.

"Give me my children, Jim," she sighed. "I only want my children. You can have the woman. This doesn't matter. Just let the children go."

Jim stepped back, his black eyes icy, and reached for his shotgun. He spoke no words, and no one moved but Anna, as he narrowed the gun to her mother's head. Lula stepped back as Jim cocked the trigger. She still pleaded and begged for her children as the first shot rang out, and Jim cocked the trigger again.

"Run, mamma!" Anna screamed, fighting against the hold of Carrie. "Run, mamma, we'll find you!"

And Lula turned. She couldn't go very fast, but she labored, dodging as the bullets sped by her, and she got smaller and smaller as she stumbled, falling through the high weeds to escape. Soon the children could see only a scrap of white dress and long hair that faded either from the horizon, or through a fall. Soon the porch was quiet, except for Lula's children's tortured sobs that meant nothing to the others. Jim, Carrie and their children went inside the house. Doc, Roosevelt, Essie and Anna stood on the porch, their eyes cried out, their hearts broken. Anna walked to the edge of the lane, where the sunflowers met her in equal. She squatted in the dirt and watched as the doodle-bugs scurried across the small patches of blood her mother had trailed. And yes, this time was truly different. For as the young girl lay in the dirt, crying her heart out to God and the world, a living part of her died. A very small child grew up inside this day, and she was engulfed by that terrible lonely feeling that was to stay with her forever. The doodlebugs jumped as the clouds moved slowly across the heavens, and Anna prayed—a child's prayer of peace for the mother she would never in life see again.

The next day Jim packed all that was possible and piled the children and his new family into the wagon. Everything was done with much haste, with much left behind. Before she left, Anna took a small doily of her mother's and stuck it in her waistband. They raced off as if running for their lives and rode most of the morning 'til they came to a high shack similar to their own.

The children sat quietly looking at the other children with whom they must now spend their lives. Anna noticed how much they favored her father; the same color, same features. She looked back at Carrie, sitting staunch and confident beside her father, and her small heart filled with hate. She knew what her path in life would be, and she meant to follow it for her mother. She meant to never let her leave her heart.

Nancy was home within a week and went to visit her family, never expecting what was to meet her. The rooms were almost empty. Everything was scattered and toppled. The children and Lula were gone. Never bothering to close the front door behind her, she walked the path to her home. Her mind raved with wonder. "Where are they? What could have happened?" She noticed the specks of blood along the way, but prayed they were from a stray animal. She climbed the stairs and sat on the porch, shaking with anticipation, fearful of the unknown.

At the other house the children carried what they could inside. Jim hitched the wagon, and Carrie scurried around barking orders to all except her own. The girls were all put in one room, and the boys were placed in the corner, beside the cold stove. They were tired and hungry, and Carrie took no time in telling Essie and the boys to open some canned goods. They ate, and as the children cleared the table, Doc and Roosevelt pulled Essie and Anna aside, promising them that they would run away and find Aunt Nancy. And somehow Anna felt better, somehow she knew her Aunt would help them. She knew Aunt Nancy would find her mother, and take them all away to live together, like it should have been so long ago. And as Anna lay on the straw pallet next to a girl her age who she didn't know, she watched the fire flies dancin' outside the window. They reminded her of her mother's hair and she felt warm. Things would be okay—things would be all right.

The broken door to the room creaked open as Carrie walked in. As she stepped over Anna to cover up her own child, Anna played sleep while Carrrie took her child from her soggy place and pushed Anna into a wet mess. She lay still as it seeped through her clothes, knowing she had no say. She watched the child sleep in the dry spot that was hers and she despised her. More, she despised Carrie. But she laid there, cold, soaked and clinging to the prayer of hope that was within her. And far into the night she'd listened as her father and Carrie's voices, drunk with whiskey, escalated. She listened as the bumps hit the wall and the tables overturned, and she smiled to know that Carrie fared no better than her mother in the battle with Jim.

The next morning Essie helped Anna off with the wet clothes and soaked them in the tub out back. Anna ran into the kitchen. She wanted to see the result of Carrie's beating. They were obvious. Carrie's eyes were swollen and lip split. Anna positioned herself directly across from Carrie at the dinner table. It was her way of gloating. All through the tense meal she watched her, and Carrie glared at the child's eyes who dared to out stare her.

With breakfast over, Jim left and Carrie began her tirade. She hauled a huge bundle of soiled laundry to the door and instructed Essie and Anna to take it out back to wash. She told Doc and Roosevelt to take reapers and cut all the surrounding weeds, then hand plow her garden. Her children stayed mostly in the house. Anna didn't know quite what they did all day, but it continued this way for a week. Carrie worked them with a fervor, only being kind and caring when Jim came home.

At the end of the week, as Anna again laid in the puddle that was not hers, Doc snuck into the room. He nudged Anna and Essie, telling them to be quiet.

"Me and Roosevelt are leaving tonight," he whispered. "We're gonna find Aunt Nancy, but we'll be back." Anna and Essie hugged their brother, knowing they were taking a big chance. Then pulling his step-sister into the wet spot on the pallet, he placed Anna on the dry spot, waved good-bye and quietly closed the door.

Sleep was hard for Essie and Anna that night. They were full of fear and anticipation for both themselves and their brothers, but they knew Aunt Nancy would help them. And in whispered conversation throughout the night, the girls soon met the sun, giggling when their step-sister woke up with a wail about being wet.

Jim raged angrily about the boys being gone. He threatened to kill them. Carrie added her two cents about Lula's childrens' ungratefulness. They questioned, even badgered the girls who kept silent. They were slapped and beaten, but they said nothing cause they knew silence was their only hope.

On about the fourth day a buggy pulled up to the house. Nancy, Doc and Roosevelt got out. Nancy walked stiffly like a marching soldier as she entered the screen never knocking. Carrie stood by the table, very quiet. She gathered her children to her and said nothing. Nancy glared at her. She walked through the house like it was hers.

"Where's Jim!" she demanded. "And where's my girls?"

Carrie never moved as Essie and Anna bounded from the back room to their Aunt. She looked down as Nancy walked about, gathering what she could of the girls things. As they headed for the wagon, Jim pulled up. They looked at each other but never spoke. And putting the children in the wagon, Nancy pulled off.

That night, after a good dinner of bacon, greens and potatoes, Nancy got the children settled for bed. When they were asleep, she sat in her chair facing the window and thought. She thought of Jim. "Well, no need to try to sort it all out now," she figured as she slowly walked to bed.

The children woke bright and early with a burst. They ate biscuits and syrup and went about their chores at Nancy's instructions. Nancy hitched the buggy and drove about hoping to find Lula. She asked around but the stories, if any, varied. At mid-day she went home to check on the children, with no more news than when she'd left. Essie had fixed a crude soup which served as lunch and Anna had arranged flowers, although mostly weeds, on the wooden table. Nancy looked around her. All was neat and in its place but she knew it couldn't last. She knew Jim would never allow them to stay, plus she was getting up in years. The children chatted noisily but their voices seemed far distant as Nancy watched them, thinking. Eating slowly, she wished Lula had drawn up papers giving her the children. She wished she had some legal stance on which to stand. She wished they were hers.

Each day passed much as the first, and the children seemed relaxed, almost happy. There were questions about their mother but Nancy had no answers, except in her heart. One night a few weeks later, the children sat around Aunt Nancy's worn chair, listening as she told them stories of long ago. She told them how it was on Buchanan Plantation, and of Jim, Fanny, Mayo and Will. She told of their grandparents and Millie and Jake. Anna's eyes brightened on the part of how her father and mother met, courted, and wed. She smiled as Aunt Nancy told of Lula's great beauty and how happy things had been. And they grew wise when told of how the men had come and taken the plantation from them like so many thieves. She listened carefully and somehow understood all the anger, whether or not it was vented in the wrong direction.

The wagon pulled up unnoticed by the children, as they were intensely listening to her stories, but Nancy heard it. She never got up to look, for she knew who it was. The knock came slowly, sharply, and Nancy opened the door. Jim walked in wearing his Sunday best. He looked almost handsome as he gave his regards to all, focusing blankly at an oval picture on the wall.

"I came to get my kids, Nancy," he started slowly, motioning for Anna to come to him. She never moved and he went on. "I know I made a lot of mistakes, but I've had some time to think. I want them back."

The room was eerily silent, as no one responded, no one moved. Jim cleared his throat uneasily. He was a proud man and felt somehow desperate, like he was losing again.

"Then, just give me Anna," he begged. "Give me the baby, and you can keep the rest."

Nancy walked slowly to her brother. She looked into eyes that were much like hers, and spoke with a calm even she didn't understand.

"Get out of my house Jim," she said, then walked to the door. Nancy stood in the doorway, leaning against the peeling wood, watching her brother walk to his wagon.

"Jim," she said, her voice stern, louder. "Where's Lula?"

Jim never turned around, he never answered, just whipped his horses to a start and drove away. Two days later he was back with the sheriff, the same sheriff who bought his moonshine, and he hauled the children back to his house and Miss Carrie.

The days and weeks lingered like months for the children, whose only joy seemed to be the visits from Aunt Nancy. She cautioned them to obey and do all they were told, and to make themselves scarce. They did. They tried to avoid Miss Carrie and the other children, who delighted in getting them beat.

After chores, Essie and Roosevelt generally played in the dirt together, while Doc, always somber and silent, found a favorite oak tree under which to whittle or read. Anna was always alone. She usually sat out back near the fence playing with the doodlebugs and flowers. She sang ditty childlike songs, often made up, and she thought of her mother.

Both boys seemed almost completely withdrawn, while Essie became more and more defiant. She hated the farm and she hated Carrie and her children and she never tried to hide it. One particular day, tensions and tempers ran high in the house. Jim had beat Carrie for no apparent reason, and the children had received the extent of all her anger after he left. She shouted and raged, barking orders, like a pit bull, to Doc and Roosevelt to walk into town for corn meal and rice. On the way back they were to stop at Bert and Sara's and bring back a hundred pound sack of potatoes, and she gave them one hour to do it. She made Anna clean and scrub the floors while Essie was told to chop kindling wood for the fire.

Essie grabbed the ax and went out to the woodpile. She seethed, as Carrie's children played, carefree and giggling with the tire swing that hung on the old oak. She boiled as they laughed at them, poking fun at Anna, calling her milky and strange. The oldest jumped from the swing and ran to the woodpile.

"Chop, Essie, chop," she teased as she ran around the pile sticking her fingers both in the way and in Essie's face. "Doesn't your little sister look cute down there cleaning up my mess?" she taunted as she smiled her ugly smile through crooked teeth. Essie kept chopping. "Where's your mama?", she giggled as she poked and played. And Essie's mind flashed, it soared. Then, aiming carefully, she brought the ax down with the skill of a woodsman, and in the growing kindling pile lay two of the girl's fingers. The screaming was deafening as the girl raced to the house, blood pouring, with her siblings in tow.

Anna ran passed them to her sister Essie as Doc and Roosevelt quickened their pace under the load of the heavy potato sack. At the kindling pile, the four laughed soundly, and then Essie kicked the chopped fingers under the water trench and walked to the house for her punishment.

And what a punishment. By the time Jim got home, Carrie had already beaten her badly, but Jim grabbed the buggy whip and lashed at Essie with no mercy. Anna watched, crying softly as the whip struck her sister time and again, red whelps rising on her body like baking biscuits. He beat her until he was tired, then threw her in the room where she lay on the floor, more mad than hurt. Anna went in to the kitchen, bringing back the alcohol and a wad of cotton. Jim was still raging, pushing the children and chairs out of his way, but she wasn't afraid. With eyes that never left him, she walked right passed him to the room and closed the door. And gently putting her sister's head in her lap she wiped her wounds with alcohol mixed with tears. Both girls cried that night, and when tears came no more, Anna whispered to Essie, "You got her good! Was it worth it?" Essie managed a slight smile and the sisters went to sleep. The whip scars would stay on Essie for the rest of her life.

With Essie out of commission for a while the workload was especially hard on the other three. But somehow there was a sense of satisfaction whenever they looked at the girl's crippled hand.

Essie was strong and in a few weeks was able to get around. She was scarred and marked horribly, but she didn't care. Somehow it all seemed worth it to her. But the battles continued, with Anna getting the brunt of most of them.

Dinner seemed always quiet, staid, but particularly quiet one day in early Autumn. Jim was restless, too restless, and the air was as a hot balloon, soon to pop. Everyone made as little noise as possible from the tin plates and cups as they ate rations of hog lights, livers, rice and biscuits. Carrie shifted uneasily in her chair, and Anna watched her, knowing the woman could only anticipate the worst. "How dare her think that she'd actually fare better than my mother?" she thought, as she watched her father scoot his chair from the table and head out the door. They heard the horses neigh and knew he was leaving but no one moved. With dinner over, Essie and Anna cleared the table, while Doc and Roosevelt filled the big tub with water for the dishes. Soon they heard their father's voice.

"I got a big run tonight," he started. "One of the biggest yet. Maybe this will help us get out of this hole we're in."

This said, he left, the screen door slamming behind him in a final statement.

The girls finished their work as quickly as possible that night. With their father gone they wanted to invite no turmoil, so they lay down early. With morning they started their usual routine, with no sight of their father, but they thought nothing of it. He was often gone for days.

On the fourth day, about ten p.m., the house was awakened, by a boisterous pounding on the door. Phil Matthew's voice boomed, "Hurry, hurry, Jim is hurt."

Everyone piled to the door as Jim stumbled in, his clothes ragged, blood oozing down his chest and shoulder. Phil half-dragged him over to the couch, and yelled for rags, water, scissors, and pliers. The children's eyes were wild as Jim lay still, silent, laboring to breathe. Phil worked on him with fervor. Sweat poured from Jim like a wrung rag, and finally came the welcome bing of the bullet as it hit the floor. Phil leaned back, sighing as he bandaged Jim. He was proud of his work even though he well knew his reputation in the small town. Many called him a quack, but he knew he was all they had, and he did the best he could.

Anna bent down and looked deeply at her father's face. It was lined now, but still handsome. He looked so peaceful, so calm, so ragged out. She bent closer 'til she felt his slight breath on her cheek. He was still alive, and for some reason she felt relief. Did she really, somehow, love him? But her moment with her father was brief. Carrie quickly snatched her out of the way and directed them to bed.

"He's my father!" Anna screamed at her, only to be slapped soundly.

"Yes, and he's my man!" Carrie retorted, with a look that only they understood, as they scampered to bed.

Days, weeks, passed and Jim was weak from his wound. The house was quieter, but no less turbulent. The children continued to rile each other with a "you do, then I do" attitude, and Carrie continued to take her children's side. It was getting cool and everyone stayed inside a lot now. Jim improved along with a lot of his temper, but without full steam. All of the children, when inside, were careful or at least sneaky enough to stay clear of his glance as much as possible. Essie was especially fidgety. Little Carrie, Miss Carrie's middle child, had taxed her last nerve. She picked at Essie, lied on her, and was intent to get her for chopping off her sister's fingers. And Little Carrie relished that one day a week when her mother took her father to Dr. Matthews. That was always her settling day. Before they left, Carrie ordered Doc and Roosevelt to go out and cut and stack kindling, and Essie to sweep and clean the fireplace, dispose of the ashes and start a fresh fire. Anna was to scrub the cast iron skillets, and Carrie's children were to assist too, but Essie and Anna knew they wouldn't.

As soon as the buggy was out of sight and the boys out of the way, Little Carrie started in. She mimicked while Essie cleaned the fireplace, singing loud songs and kicking the ashes. Essie kept working. Anna watched from the kitchen, banging the pots in defiance. Little Carrie headed for the kitchen, but stopped short when the boys brought in a load of kindling. Piling it high they went back out to chop, and Essie commenced to put the wood in the fireplace, dousing it with kerosene. Taking a long wooden match, she lit the fire, poking at it slowly, as it grew and danced in her eyes. She seemed almost lost in the flames.

    Anna continued her work in the kitchen. It was quiet. She figured the spat had died down, but she turned only to find Little Carrie behind her holding a paper bag filled with soot and ashes. She stood laughing as she dumped them in clean pots. Anna grabbed the rag and lashed at her, again and again, but she was no match for the bigger girl. Little Carrie smacked Anna into the living room, racing after her like a headless hen. Essie turned around, the light from the fire dancin' in her eyes, the red hot poker in her hand. Stepping between them, she lashed at Little Carrie with the poker, burning her again and again between the legs. Even as she fell to the floor, Essie continued to burn her there 'til the flesh singed and hung with the stench of burning skin. Anna screamed; over and over she screamed, as she pulled at her sister and the poker. Essie sat back and watched as Little Carrie writhed on the floor, crying, burning, but her victory was short lived.

    The buggy rolled to a stop just as the boys reached the front door, and the sisters looked at each other, not with fear, but with knowing. Doc whispered to Essie, "Why? Why?", but Jim and Miss Carrie were already in the room. She screamed a curdling noise that seemed to rock the house, and they both looked at Essie, who still stood with the poker in hand. Jim walked slowly to Essie as Anna jumped in front, but he pushed her aside, landing a blow that sent Essie reeling to the front door. Then, grabbing her by the hair, he pulled Essie outside to the well where he tied her arms and hung her. Jim walked away and never looked back, as Anna stood on the porch crying, Essie was in the well, she was hanging in the well, and Anna could do nothing about it. She looked inside as Carrie rubbed salve on her daughter's thighs and privates that were blistered and black. Then she walked to the well to sit.

"Essie," she called down in the hole that seemed endless.

"I'm okay," was the reply. "Just stay with me."

And Anna did. It seemed like hours that she sat there, with Doc and Roosevelt checking every so often. Jim never came out to check her.

Anna was cold and hungry, but she knew there'd be no dinner today. She didn't care. Essie was in the well, and she felt guilty. Pulling her cotton dress about her, the sisters whispered this and that to each other and time passed. The air was almost chilling, and Essie kept urging Anna to go inside, but she wouldn't budge. She just sat and consoled her sister, never noticing the buggy that had pulled up to the side of the house.

It was Aunt Nancy. It's funny how she always turned up at the right time. Doc and Roosevelt met her at the back door, whispering what had happened, and Essie's fate. Marching through the house, Nancy looked at Jim, then Carrie, who held her whimpering daughter to her. She marched right through the house and out the front door to the well, with Doc and Roosevelt in tow. She saw Anna huddled by the well and looked down to see small arms criss-crossed, bound in rope. She reeled Essie up, her arms weary and bleeding from the bondage. She held Essie, and Essie did not pull away. She was so stiff she could barely walk, and she leaned on her aunt like a crutch. When they got back in the house, she directed the children to get some warm clothes, and announced to her brother they were going with her.

Jim was quiet and then said, "You know the law's on my side, Nancy. You have no rights here, but you can have them. All but Anna. She stays with us." The room was silent, and then finally Anna spoke up.

"Please take them with you," she said to her Aunt. "I'll be okay!"

The children packed quietly as they cried. Nancy's face was somber as she watched all in silence. Anna went out to the porch and sat on the high steps looking out over the fields. Her eyes kept filling but she was careful to brush the tears away. It was chilly, night was coming and Anna ached. She felt like she did as she'd watched her mother being driven away. She dropped her head in her lap as the screen door opened, and Nancy and the children came out. They all hugged Anna and promised to be back for her, but somehow things felt different this time. Nancy held her close. She whispered words of hope as Anna clasped Essie's hands. The boys put the bags in the buggy and Nancy pulled Essie away into the wagon. With a click the horses pulled off and Anna was left alone. And she cried. Sinking beside a barren tree, she cried as the buggy drifted out of sight. It was night now and she sat a long time in her solitude. Finally her father came to the porch and called.

He was leaning against the rail inside, waiting, as she slowly climbed the stairs. He picked her up and looked in her eyes, which were red and swollen, then carried her inside, and sat in the over-stuffed chair, holding her small hand, almost marveling at its perfect grace. He knew she was hurting, but he never was quite good with these kinds of words. So he held her, and soon Anna fell asleep, with all that was left in her tiny world.

The next morning Anna awoke early and climbed from her father's lap. He was still asleep, so she ran to the room to get a blanket to cover him. As Carrie and her daughter were asleep in her bed, she sat by the fireplace and placed some logs to make a fire. Lying on the floor, she watched the flames. How they danced so brightly and uncaring. How she wished she could dance this way. Her mind drifted to better times, and yes, there were some. There were times of love and play with her mother, games she'd played with her sister and brothers, and even hunting with her father, or just watching him build his stills or kill chickens. But her memories were short-lived. Miss Carrie and several of her children bounded into the room, talking much louder than anybody should this early in the morning. And Anna knew her day was beginning.

And what a day it was. Her mind drifted so much to her sister and brothers that she was often yelled at for not listening. She was glad her father was home, cause Miss Carrie always treated her better. It was that night she dreaded. She knew she had to go back in that room to sleep with the others. Still, Aunt Nancy's words of hope filtered through her mind, and with her chores done, about mid-day she pulled her over large sweater about her and crawled beneath the high porch. She looked for doodle-bugs to play with but they were long since gone—being so cold and all. Grabbing a stick she started to write and memorize all the lessons Aunt Nancy had taught her. She put them together in words and sentences and rhyme. She became lost in herself, like the people in the house didn't exist, but still the tears came. They mingled with her words and smeared them as the ground got wet. Anna didn't want to cry, but she was so lonely, so empty, so lost.

"Anna!" Miss Carrie screamed, her voice cutting the air like ragged pinking shears. Anna jumped. It was almost night, and she knew she was gonna get it for not helping with dinner. She scrambled from beneath the porch, up the stairs and into the house. Miss Carrie stood by the door with an odd smile on her face.

"Sit down dear," she said. "Dinner is ready."

Anna figured the woman had been dipping in her father's whiskey, but she said nothing. And easing into a chair, she ate her biscuits and gravy, in silence.

The days dragged. They seemed like weeks. Anna did all that was told, then slipped off to herself. She was thankful that her father still wasn't well enough to leave yet, and she avoided Miss Carrie and the others as much as possible. She learned to ignore the remarks, and to ignore Miss Carrie's grins even more. On many afternoons she either sat under the porch, wandered about the yard, or climbed the rickety fence to sing lonely songs to the cucumbers.

Winter was quickly approaching, and one day as Anna hung on the fence, her father told her to run in and put on a decent dress. She was going to school. Anna ran to the house, changed into the best she had and raced to the buggy, careful to smile over her shoulder at the others. Her father was waiting in the wagon and as Anna climbed up, he handed her a lard bucket and a box. She opened the box. Shoes! A pair of new shoes. She hurriedly discarded her worn ones and put on the new. They were a little tight, but it didn't matter. They were new. Opening the small bucket, she neatly arranged her lunch of corn bread and syrup. Anna was going to school, and she looked at her father and smiled. He nodded his head at her and she smiled. Maybe he did love her.

And Anna's days were brighter. She caught on quickly in the small one room school, and the teacher liked her. She knew Anna was different and kind. The other children basically ignored her, but it didn't matter, for she quickly became the teacher's pet. As often as possible she stayed after school to learn more, even if it meant getting in trouble.

The times when Aunt Nancy brought Essie and the others over they gathered around Anna to hear the news of school. Carrie's children hung in the background envious of the attention given to Anna, and she relished it. For she was the only one of Jim's children he'd allowed to go to school.

Winter had set in, and it was bitter. Jim was better off and back to work in the fields and with his still. Every morning Anna took the buggy ride with him to school but she didn't mind the cold. She held her tattered books and papers to her, clickin' her new shoes to the horses stride.

Thanksgiving came and Jim allowed Anna to spend the day at Aunt Nancy's. They had a goose, some butter beans and biscuits, and Nancy made some rich pumpkin pies from a neighbor's patch. What fun they had. Sure there were dishes and clean up, but everything just seemed so right. The only thing missing was their mother. Essie asked if they were still putting the salve on little Carrie's legs, and the children roared. But all too soon, Jim was there to get her, and Anna left them, her heart sad; the only consolation being that she would be in school the next day.

The snow was packed on the grounds of the little one-room school, and recess was a welcome time for the children. They raced around like crazy, while Anna usually stayed behind in class with Miss Teal, or stood out by the fence to watch them. But today, she felt good inside. She'd had a nice Thanksgiving holiday with her family, and Miss Teal said she was going to give her a paper of merit for her learning. She smiled against the chilling sun and ran for the slide. She waited in line behind the other children, and then she went down it. How free she felt, and she giggled inside as she went down again and again. Then she ran to the swings to wait her turn. The other children didn't even notice her and she felt good. Climbing on the too big swing she dug her feet into the ground to push off. And off she went, into the air like a flighty bird, and the wind burned her cheeks, turning them as red as her nose. She was lost in herself and her glide and her school, so she never noticed when the children started pushing her higher, higher and higher until she was way past the metal bar, and over she went, flipping through the air like a tossed coin, onto the snowy ground. The children grew silent, the swing creaked to a stop and Miss Teal came out yelling for one of the boys to get the buggy and go after her father. Anna lay in a pile, looking around her. Her head hurt, and her leg was throbbing. Miss Teal covered her with a blanket and sent the other children inside as Jim pulled up, his face set like a dime store Indian.

Gently, he placed Anna in the back of the wagon as Miss Teal explained that the children were only playing and had pushed her a little too hard in the swing. Jim faced her.

"Get me her belongings," he said, his face holding the same expression. "She won't be coming back." And Anna sank back into the wagon, her eyes tearing, a lump in her throat—for she knew she was right back where she'd started in the first place.

Every day was much the same for Anna. Her father was again himself, and the beatings of Carrie and their children resumed. Anna missed school terribly, and savored the books, hoping one day to return. Jim sensed her sadness and tried to appear kinder to her, but still he was steadfast in his decision. His manner to Anna infuriated Carrie and she struck back every chance she got.

About a week or so after Thanksgiving Anna watched one morning as her father headed out across the fields. Miss Carrie was outside boiling clothes in the big black pot, and she called to Anna as soon as Jim was out of sight. It had snowed the night before and Anna grabbed her warm coat, and pulled it tightly about her as she went outside. Carrie put down the big stick she used for stirring the clothes and faced Anna.

"What took you so long?" she asked, her face as stern and blank as a portrait. Anna stared at her just blankly.

"It's cold. I stopped to get my coat, Miss Carrie," she answered, her young eyes never leaving the older face.

"You call me Mamma!" the woman screamed, her eyes widening. "From now on you call me Mamma!" Anna stepped back as if she'd been struck. She blinked. Surely this woman must be drugged to suggest such a thing.

"I won't do it," she replied. "I know who my Mamma is." And the blows came again and again as Carrie beat Anna about the yard. Finally Anna ran and hid under the porch. Crouching in the farthest corner, she huddled with her pain and the biting winds, and slowly morning passed; then afternoon, and she heard the creak of her father's buggy pulling up out front. Racing to it, she told him what had happened and they both marched in the house. He was furious and proceeded to give Carrie more than a sample of what she'd given Anna, and Anna felt revenged. That night the other children were silent with her, for they knew she was the cause of their mother's beating. And she relished it as she snuggled beneath her blanket to sleep.

The next day was much like the previous one. Carrie beat Anna, then when Jim came home Anna told, and he beat Carrie. This went on for about a week or so, until Jim, tired of all the mess, took Anna and moved to a friend's. It was crowded in the house but Anna was treated fairly well.

A few days later Carrie came, her eyes red and face swollen. Anna watched as Carrie focused on the hardwood floor while she begged Jim back. She listened as Carrie promised never to beat Anna again, and soon they were packing, heading back to the house she hated so. But Carrie kept her promise. She didn't beat Anna anymore. She starved her instead, refusing to feed her when Jim was not home. Then when Jim was there and Carrie offered her food, Anna was too rebellious to eat it. So the battle continued.

Christmas was near, and everyone knew it would be scarce, but tempers seemed to be a little better. Anna knew her father wasn't gonna work all day, as he had on his best clothes, and she also knew that meant he'd be drinking all day with his friends. She resented the fact that he would do this on Christmas Eve, leaving her alone with these others, who took great delight in having fun without her.

Determined to wait up for him, she sat on a tall stool in the kitchen, far into the night, 'til she heard him coming home. But who could miss him. He was roaring drunk, stumbling, swearing and Anna raged inside.

When he came into the kitchen, Anna asked, "Why, Daddy? Why?"

Jim stiffened. Then he walked over to the stool and slapped her, sending her reeling off the seat. Racing past him, she got her blanket and made a pallet by the fireplace as Jim sank like lead into a kitchen chair. Anna lay still, her feelings more hurt than her face, thankful that the others had not seen. Playing asleep she watched her father and in an hour or so he came towards her, with something in his hand. It was a stocking. Lying very still she peeked as he quietly filled it with an apple, candy and other goodies, then placed a small gift on top. Her heart warmed, but she said nothing, and once again she felt good inside. When her father had gone to bed she peeked in the stocking, filled her mouth with lemon drops, then snuggled back under her cover. She'd forgiven him for the slap even before the stocking, for she knew she needed someone to love, so she drifted to sleep. It was to be the one and only time her father would hit her.

The winter was hard for the Buchanans, but they managed, as they always did. Nothing changed, nothing passed, only time. Some of the chill had gone from the wind and Jim was once again hunting, often taking Anna with him. It seemed easier than leaving her at home. He appeared happier, freer, out in the woods, shooting at the rabbits and possums. The gunshot rang like tin bells against the still and Anna covered her ears against their peal.

One particularly clear day, Anna stood on the edge of the field watching her father and the other men as they worked. Over and over there was a booming sound, a muffled boom that was almost beckoning to a young mind.

Walking closer, Anna could see they were blowing up stumps, and as they broke for lunch, she ran to the stump clearing, full of curiosity. Beside a large tree lay a small box, and she picked it up knowing the booms came from within. Picking up a wooden match, she opened the box, her pulse racing with the sounds and danger it held. Striking the match she lit the dynamite caps, panicked, dropped the box, and ran, but not far enough. The booming noise was deafening as the blast flung her across the field, spewing pain like hot pepper though her body. Half running, half crawling Anna headed to the house, her small body aching, her legs and arms bleeding. But everyone was gone. The house was eerily silent as she stumbled to the bedroom. Then kneeling by the bed Anna prayed. She prayed to God not to let her die without seeing Aunt Nancy and the others again. She prayed to God to heal her wounds, spare her, and help her find happiness. She thanked God for her life. This was Anna's first real prayer. Then crawling into bed, she laid there, waiting, for what she wasn't sure, and soon she passed out. When her father and the others came home, that's where they found her.

    Two days later, Aunt Nancy appeared at Jim's door. She was not sent for, there was no message, but she felt that something was wrong. Nancy asked Jim where Anna was and he pointed out back, where she found her sitting on a log, all bandaged up.

    "Come with me, Anna," she said softly, reaching for her hand. "You're going home."

Nancy took Anna into the house and instructed her to get her things. Jim stood up, but Nancy started talking slowly. "I was going through some boxes and things that Lula left in the house. I found this." Then reaching for a faded piece of paper she proceeded to read. It seems Lula had papers drawn up giving custody of the children to Nancy in case something happened to her. At the bottom was the X that Lula had signed for her signature. The X that marked her children's freedom. Staring out the window, Jim never moved. Nancy and Anna walked right passed him, out the door, and still he sat. And as they drove down the path in the lopsided buggy, Anna clutched the crumbled paper, crying, staring at the X, knowing she'd remember it for the rest of her life.

Anna was going back to her family. Wiping her eyes she stared out across the fields as they neared Aunt Nancy's house. Ahead she saw Doc and Roosevelt working in the yard as Essie ran up to the buggy. The girls embraced, jumping about like rabbits startled by a sudden sound.

She settled in, putting her scant belongings in a corner against the wall. Nancy checked her wounds, then sent all the children out to play. And they played—wearing themselves out with games and chases and rambling talk of the past. They knew they'd better relish this day, because tomorrow life would be back to normal. Complete with chores.

At dinner they sat around the wooden table, and after saying grace, dug into rice, gravy and corn bread. Aunt Nancy poured them all cool glasses of buttermilk, and Anna and Essie grinned at each other across the table. Anna was happy, for this is where she belonged, and warmness filled her as she watched the portly woman with the dancin' eyes.

After a hasty clean up the children headed for bed; the girls making pallets in one corner of the room, the boys in the other. Anna knew her Aunt was gettin' older. She knew she wasn't well, and inside her young heart vowed to help in any way that she could.

The next thing Anna remembered it was morning, cool and crisp as only the country can be. Doc and Roosevelt were dressed and the girls hurried to get dressed for breakfast. Aunt Nancy had made pancakes, hot and steaming with warm maple syrup she'd made from maple flavoring and sugar and water. Nancy explained to the children that she'd agreed to cook for different people in order to make ends meet, and the girls were to assist, while the boys did their usual chores outside. It seemed like all Aunt Nancy did was work, and Anna felt somewhat sad because she knew it was for all for them.

People came and went, bringing ingredients, picking up food, then bringing laundry and clothes to iron. The days, weeks were filled with a lot of work, but a lot of love, and time passed. Essie and Aunt Nancy did most of the work, but Anna helped whenever she could.

The boys worked the small fields, fed the cow and the few chickens they had, and sometimes Anna wandered outside to watch. Doc and Roosevelt figured she was more in the way than anything else so they usually sent her to the hen house to play with the chickens. Anna liked the hens and would chase them, singing made up songs while they fluttered in disarray. At feeding time she ate too, grabbing handfuls of the cracked corn. She loved it, and ate scads of it everyday, counting the crunches it took to swallow.

Well, times were hard, and usually a bag of feed lasted months. Nancy began noticing it's disappearance, but said nothing.

One particularly warm evening the children buzzed around the kitchen. It seemed Mrs. Reed had given Nancy a meaty slab of roast in payment for a meal she had cooked her, and Nancy was fixing it for the children's supper. Telling the children to be seated, she cut the meat, smothered with browned potatoes, and brought the plates to the table. She sat a plate before the boys, then Essie, then went back for hers and Anna's. Anna was shocked. On her plate was a huge, brimming pile of cracked corn. Sitting at her place Nancy instructed the children to say their blessing and eat, and they did as they were instructed. Anna's heart sank but she ate every bite of the feed, saying nothing when her Aunt filled the plate again. Her stomach ached and she felt like the cracked corn was coming out of her ears, but she ate it, rolling her eyes at her sister who ate her fine dinner with an elfin smile on her face. Needless to say, Anna never ate the chicken's feed again.

Each day passed much like the first on the small farm, but Anna was happy. She knew Aunt Nancy loved them but was adamant about their obedience. It seems like Aunt Nancy was moving a little slower these days and they all knew she was working far too hard.

Down the way was a small grocery store run by a kindly man everyone called *Cheese*. Cheese knew that times were hard for Nancy trying to raise four young children so he offered her a tab for groceries, allowing her to pay him when the folks she worked for paid her. This seemed to work out well and Nancy was always sure to pay her bill on time. This way she could get small treats for the children once in a while, like oranges and grapefruits. She'd core the fruits and serve them at breakfast, then candy the rinds for a treat after dinner, and the children loved them.

Anna had been there some months now and the newness of her arrival had settled in. The boys, still distant and quiet, kept mostly to themselves with Essie usually tormenting them 'til they allowed her to play. Anna, not quite as pushy, again found herself on the sidelines, with the others believing her too young to join in. But this didn't matter, for she was home, so she'd watch them play, while she sang her made-up words to the chickens and doodle-bugs. And sometimes, when Aunt Nancy needed something from the grocery, they'd let her tag along; feeling important, she walked about the stores many shelves.

One warm afternoon, when all the chores were done, Anna wandered outside, around back, looking for her brothers and sister. For about a week or so she'd been building a tiny hut out of twigs and paste, topping the roof with flower petals and cloth and she wanted to show them.

She'd cut people out of paper, and with small rocks made furniture and she was proud of it. She even thought that maybe they'd want to play with her.

As she bent over her perfect job, Essie came up behind her, a slight grin on her perfect face. Doc and Roosevelt stood behind her, grinning and commenting on what a great job she had done, when Essie spoke up.

"You know what your house needs?" she asked, looking back at the boys. "It needs some treats, little cakes or something to put inside. We'll even play with you if you come down to Cheese's store with us to get some stuff." Anna jumped up and the children headed for the grocery, Essie in the lead. Once out front the others sent Anna in, assuring her that Aunt Nancy wouldn't care because it was for a game. Anna went inside.

The store seemed huge, the few aisles extra long as Anna walked about trying to decide. Finally she picked out some candy sticks, crackers and caramel and headed for the counter, where Cheese met her with a smile.

"My Aunt Nancy sent me," she started. "She says to just put them on her bill."

Cheese added the items and wrote them down, thanking Anna as she scurried out of the store. A horrible guilt came over her, but she knew it would make her brothers and sister happy.

Outside the others were quick to grab the loot, but slow on sharing it, but Anna didn't mind. All she got was a cracker and a piece of caramel, which she ate slowly as the others ran on up ahead of her. When they reached Aunt

Nancy's the children ran off toward the field, and Anna sat down at her playhouse. They never did come back to join her.

The next day was a repeat performance. She was coerced to go to Cheese's store and charge things and generally ended up playing alone. This went on for a while.

On Saturday nights Aunt Nancy always cooked Sunday dinner, for Sunday was not cooking time. It was church time.

This one particular Saturday night, Aunt Nancy, tired from a long working day, stood by the hot stove, her brow slightly sweating, her eyes tired. A knock came, and Doc ran to the door, edging it open, and there stood Cheese.

Stepping into the living room he greeted all and proceeded into the kitchen.

"Nancy?" he asked. "When are you gonna take care of your bill? I'm not trying to push you, but it's starting to add up, and anything that you can settle will help."

Nancy turned around.

"But I don't owe you anything, Cheese!" she answered, her eyes curious.

"Well," Cheese continued, "your youngest girl here has been in the store practically every night charging stuff, she said was for you. I only allowed it cause they're your children."

Nancy's voice lowered. "I'll take care of it," she said, turning full attention to the children. " You'll be paid." Closing the door behind Cheese, Nancy wiped her hands on her apron.

The children looked from one to the other not even trying to hide their fear. Shaking, they watched as their Aunt reached for the razor strap that hung on a nail by the back door. They knew what this meant. Anna was petrified, for she knew she was the only one Cheese had mentioned, so she spoke up. Aunt Nancy told them all to take their positions on the floor, according to age, face down, rear-ends exposed. Starting with Doc, and going down the line, she whipped them, but was careful to skip Anna every other lick. Well, she whipped a while, sat a while, cooked a while, and then whipped some more that evening. She really made a night of it, and that next morning, sore and tired, the children sat, or attempted to sit, in church. Charging goodies at Cheese's grocery was the last thing on their minds.

The thing now was trying to figure out how to pay Cheese off, and finally, after checking with a few farmers, Doc and Roosevelt, as the oldest, were made to pull fodder to pay the bill. Every morning for what seemed like quite a while, Nancy got the boys up at dawn and on their way. A little after sun set usually found them coming home, tired, but all the better for it. The bill was slowly being paid.

One day, as the sun slowly set, Anna ran out by the fence to wait for her brothers. It seems Cheese had told Aunt Nancy he'd let them work cleaning up the store and filling bins or running errands, and she wanted to be the first to tell them. The sun went down. Still she waited, but they did not come. Anna started thinking. That morning before the boys had left, she remembered they'd awakened her and Essie. Usually they just left, but this morning they'd said good-bye.

Anna walked back to the house and was met on the porch by her Aunt and sister. Her eyes watering, she said, almost in a whisper, "They're not coming back."

Hitching the buggy, Nancy and the girls rode to the boys' job site. They were met by a kindly farmer named Zolio. Nancy figured him and his wife Julia were Spanish cause they talked differently than the other folks around. But they were good people who settled among them with no problems, and were well liked.

"I came to get my boys," Nancy told them. "Are they done yet?"

Zolio helped her from the wagon. "They're gone Nancy. They left some time ago, after they were paid. I was just on my way to tell you. They told Jose they were going up North."

Nancy stiffened but she said nothing.

"Would you like some coffee?" Julia asked, but Nancy touched her hand and said no and climbed back in the wagon.

"Wait!" said Zolio. "They left this for you." He handed Nancy a white envelope, which she opened. Inside was the money they had earned and a small note saying, "We love you, but we had to go, Aunt Nancy. Life is gonna be better soon. Please tell the girls good-bye." Anna cried, and even Essie fought back the tears she wanted no one to see.

Nancy clicked the horses to a start. Zolio told her, "They're good boys Nancy. Good hard working boys. They'll make it."

Then the buggy headed down the path to home, slowly, with no words spoken. Clutching the crumbled paper, Anna stared out over the darkened fields. Again she cried; openly, thinking, remembering. And Anna would never see her brothers, Doc or Roosevelt, again.

Times were much harder now on the little farm, with the boys gone. Everything; food, fodder, cooking, feeding; everything, had to be done by Nancy and the girls, and things were dwindling fast. Nancy's hands just didn't seem to work like they used to and they were swelled and red with arthritis. The girls noticed her legs and feet were always swollen and she coughed a lot, but she kept going. Not as fast as before, but she kept going. Anna wondered just when these things started happening, or were they really happening all along and she hadn't noticed.

Essie and Anna both missed the boys terribly and not a day passed that they didn't talk of them. One day as the girls were out back, feeding the chickens, Essie admitted to Anna that she was somewhat envious of the boys having gone.

"Just think," Essie told her. "They can go where they want, and do what they want. They probably got real good jobs making scads of money, and they're free." Anna listened, but somehow she just did not feel envy. All she knew was that she missed them, and wished they'd come home.

Weeks passed and nothing got any better. One particular Saturday, Nancy stood by the hot stove pouring hot gravy into tin bowls, when Essie ran in, shouting that old man Reed had offered to buy a couple of the fattest chickens, but Nancy did not answer. She did not turn around. Both girls had noticed she'd been especially quiet the last few days, and they hadn't questioned it. But Anna felt scared inside. She had that same jumping scary feeling she always got when she was gonna lose someone she loved.

After they'd sat down and said their blessings, Essie asked her, again, about the chickens. Her aunt half looked at her, instructing her to take the best two over after dinner, and silence returned.

Finally looking up from her untouched plate, Nancy cleared her throat. "Girls" she said slowly, as if choosing her words. "You know that times are hard, the worst they've ever been. We cannot make ends meet, and my health is such that I can't do much anymore. You girls need so much more. Since you're the oldest Essie, I've made arrangements to send you to a little school called Lumpkin. It's some miles away and you'll be living with the people who run the school. You'll work for them to earn your keep. They seem like decent enough folks, and it's a way for you to learn some things, and earn a little money—besides, Essie, it's the only way. You leave tomorrow."

Anna looked up from her bowl of gravy, which had cooled from her dropping tears. Both Essie and Aunt Nancy were wiping their eyes as she called her girls to her. Brushing back their hair, and their tears, she assured them over and over again that they were loved, but there was just no other way.

No dishes were done that night. Nancy packed Essie's few belongings, and the girls sat huddled at the foot of the old rocker, crying, and whispering promises through the night.

With morning, Anna helped Essie gather her things and stood out on the porch with her while their Aunt hitched up the buggy. When they were ready to go Nancy told Anna she must stay to look after things, but Anna knew the real reason.

The buggy pulled away. Anna stood on the edge of the path and watched. Essie turned around in the buggy and watched Anna. The dust clouded their view, but still the girls watched, crying, waving, hesitant to say good-by. The buggy disappeared, and still Anna stood by the path for a long time. The sun beat down and certain birds sang their song, but for whom? She looked around the yard, which was ragged and still, and in her mind's eye she saw Essie, Doc and Roosevelt runnin' about. Walking to the fence, she looked at the tiny house she'd built of sticks and she took it apart. No need for it now, no need for anything, she thought as she ran to get under the porch.

"Doodle-bugs, where are you today?" she wondered. "You're the only friends I have now," she cried, as once more that terrible, overwhelming feeling of loneliness engulfed her. So Anna lay in the dirt beneath the porch, crying, her tears making tiny wet patches where they dropped. And almost two days later, when Aunt Nancy came home that's where she found her.

Essie wrote to Anna whenever she could, which wasn't often. The letters only served to make things worse, as they told how lonely and unhappy she was at Lumpkin. Anna would read and re-read the letters, which she kept in an old shoe box in the closet.

The days and weeks passed slowly. To Anna, Aunt Nancy seemed so much older than before, but still she tried to make do. The house was so quiet now, especially at night, that you could actually count the drips from the rusty bucket in the kitchen. Nancy generally sat and sewed clothes to sell, and Anna would sit by the fire and read books or Essie's letters. In bed she usually cried herself to sleep.

In the day time Anna did all she was told to help out, like carrying water, or kneading dough, or taking cooked meals to the neighbors. She washed dishes and brought in kindling, but usually her Aunt just scooted her outside.

There she'd play her games; the lonely games that she knew only too well. She'd sing her songs to the cucumbers and flowers, and make the doodlebugs jump at will, and she'd dream. She knew there was no need to feel too sorry for herself. Besides, she'd almost made up her mind that this was her lot. Oh, she knew Aunt Nancy loved her, but she was still so very sad—so very lonely.

Then one day, there came a knock—that dreaded knock, near dusk, that always seemed to bring dread. It was a clear, crisp early evening, and everything was particularly quiet. Nancy got the door with Anna close behind her, and was met by a thin white man in a too tight suit.

"Nancy Buchanan?" he asked. She nodded, and he handed her a piece of paper, then turned and walked away.

Nancy went to her rocker and sat, opening the paper slowly. Then she read it, folded it up and sat back. Anna's curiosity was killing her, but Aunt Nancy said nothing for a while. Then she spoke, and with words Anna knew she was choosing.

"Your Pa is taking us to court," she started. "It seems he wants you back. He wants you to live with him and Carrie." Anna blinked and closed her eyes.

"No! No! No!" her small mind screamed. "Please, Jesus, don't let this happen." Her face reddened but she did not cry. She was angry. Angry at her life, at all of the desertion, at the folded piece of paper. This was not fair, life was not fair. Aunt Nancy put Anna's head on her knee and stroked her hair.

"Don't worry, I won't let you go back." And in Anna the rage subsided some, but the doubt remained.

The day of court was unusually warm for this time of year. Anna had on her best dress, a cotton frock, that Aunt Nancy had made her for this occasion. Her red hair was combed back in a black ribbon, and her pale face shone from its scrubbing. Aunt Nancy, with her loose suit and flowered hat, walked beside her, holding her hand. There was a lump in Anna's throat. A lump she could not swallow.

The court house was muggy, like there were too many different bodies inside, and Anna's eyes darted as they entered the courtroom and immediately met her father's. He sat there, straight and proper beside Miss Carrie and her step sisters and brothers, like they were a perfect family. Anna thought they looked like brown statues. She and Aunt Nancy took their seat, and soon the judge came in. They all stood and Anna looked over. She wondered if her stepsister's hands or other parts were any better from Essie's wrath, and she giggled inside.

Once seated, the judge read some papers. Then he called Miss Carrie to the stand. Anna wanted to gag, as she listened to all the lies of how much she was loved. She squeezed her Aunt Nancy's hand as she listened to Miss Carrie proclaim that all she wanted was to be a good mother to her.

Anna's mind raced, "But you're not my mother, you'll never be," and she stared at the woman squarely in the eyes.

Her father took the stand. He appeared nervous in his worn but neat suit, his dark face smooth but taunt. Their eyes met and she felt a pang of sadness in her stomach. She listened to his voice, which seemed muffled through her thoughts.

"All we want is our little girl back," he spoke, fingering the fob that hung loosely from his vest. "You see your honor, she is the youngest of me and the wife's children, and my sister Nancy had no business taking her and runnin' like that. We only want Anna back home with us."

Anna's eyes widened. "No, no!" she thought.

"Why doesn't he mention my mother? I'm not Miss Carrie's. I'm Lula Buchanan's, and he's afraid to say it 'cause he killed her."

Her mind raged, but she was silent, as Aunt Nancy tightened her grip on her hand.

The judge looked stern, a few wrinkles dug between his brow as he paused a minute.

"Mr. Buchanan," he started, as he looked at Carrie and the other children, "are all these children yours?"

"Yes your honor," her father answered.

"And Anna, is she yours too?"

"Yes your honor," he again responded. The judge looked at her and Anna was aware that she stood out like a sore thumb among the ebony faces.

"That will be all. You may step down," the judge said, and her father left the stand, Anna's eyes on his every stride.

"The court calls Nancy Buchanan to the stand," the bailiff shouted, and Nancy rose to take the chair. Her deep-set eyes seemed to be on fire as she answered all questions asked of her. Then the judge asked Nancy why she was in possession of Anna.

"Because, your honor," Nancy paused for a moment to collect her thoughts, "she's not my brother's. Why, just look at her, your honor. Skin white as milk, fiery red hair, freckles. She's not his. I took the child as a way to better her life and because I love her. And she loves me."

Nancy looked at Jim square in the eyes as he tensed, his jaw tightened, but he offered no protest. He knew if he did, that the question of Lula would come up and Nancy would surely tell all.

"You may step down," the judge offered, and Nancy straightened her bonnet and walked to her seat.

"Court will recess for one hour," said the judge. He banged his gavel and left the bench.

Small mutterings arose in the courtroom. Anna stared straight ahead at the wall as she fidgeted in her chair. She knew people were watching her and she felt nervous, uncomfortable. How she wished Essie or Doc or Roosevelt were here with her.

"Don't you worry none," her Aunt whispered to her as she gently patted her small hand. "If God's willing, everything will be all right."

The hour seemed to stretch into days. Anna was thirsty and her starchy dress was sticking her neck. Then finally the door opened, and they rose as the judge re-entered the room. A piece of paper was handed to the bailiff, who announced, *"Anna Buchanan to the stand."* Anna stiffened. Her stomach felt like the time Cheese's big dog chased her home from the store. Swallowing hard, she squeezed Aunt Nancy's hand and went to be sworn in. The chair seemed enormous and she felt lost in it. The judge was looking at her closely and it made the silence all the more intense. Picking at her fingernails, she tried to blot things by thinking of the doodlebug song as she kept her eyes trained on her Aunt.

Finally the judge cleared his throat.

"Anna," he started, "I've heard a lot of testimony here today, and I guess the end result lies with you. I'm going to ask you a simple question, and I want your honest answer to it. Who do you want to live with?"

Anna looked down at her hands. She knew she must not let the memory of a new pair of shoes, or one Christmas stocking cloud her decision. Besides, she knew that the pain and agony had far outweighed every good thing that ever happened there. She looked at her Aunt Nancy, then her father, and then she thought of her mother. The courtroom was quiet, and suddenly she was aware that everyone there was waiting for her answer. With a feeling of satisfaction, she answered clearly, loudly and smiling as her eyes danced across her face. She beamed.

"I want to live with my Aunt Nancy. I love her, and I know she loves me. That's the only place I belong." And she paused.

"You may step down now," the judge told her. Again he left the room.

Soon he was back, and the court was silent, waiting. Anna closed her eyes and said a prayer, for she knew what going back would mean for her now.

"Mr. Buchanan, Anna Buchanan, would you please rise?" They did, and he continued— his voice steady and low. "I have reached a decision in this case, for three reasons, which I will try to explain to you, Mr. Buchanan, at this time. First, the child has stated her preference for living with the defendant; secondly, the defendant, your own sister, has sworn on this court that the child is not yours; and thirdly, I'm positive within myself that Anna is not your child. Why, just look at her. She's almost white, and that's in stark contrast to you and your wife's other children. Therefore, it is my decision, and it is final, that Nancy Buchanan is hereby granted custody of said child. Anna, you may leave with your Aunt and this case is closed."

Anna and her Aunt Nancy hugged and left the courtroom hand in hand as Jim stood rigid, like any dime store Indian. Anna looked back only once as they went out the door to their wagon. The air was crisp now, almost stinging, and Anna remembered how hot it was in the courtroom. She felt good—like maybe somewhere there was a small ray of hope, of happiness. How she wished Essie and the others could see her now.

When they got home, Aunt Nancy got busy. She grabbed a few things in the short time they had and rushed Anna back to the wagon.

"We have to hurry," she told Anna, once on board. "You know your Daddy doesn't take a liking to losing, especially you, and I'm just getting too old, too tired to fight him. We have to go to another area or he'll kill us both for sure, but don't you fret none—crawl in the back and get some rest. We have a long road ahead of us."

Anna climbed to the back of the wagon, all of their happiness suddenly shattered. Snuggling beneath a blanket, she watched the trees and clouds pass above her and soon she was lulled to sleep. A sleep with tortured dreams—dreams of runnin', always runnin', dreams of guns, smoke, and shouting—dreams of her father. And she snapped herself back to reality, for she was afraid of him too. It hit her that she was really afraid of her father.

And the runnin' continued, as did the dreams. As soon as Anna figured they were settled, they'd have to pick up and leave again, as Jim was either rumored, or sighted or imagined near by. The fear was gripping, horrifying, and Anna knew there'd come a time when they could run no more.

One day Aunt Nancy neatly folded her few clothes and put them in a box. Anna thought, "I'll feel better when Aunt Nancy gets her things together too." But she didn't. Only Anna's things were being readied, so she knew what that meant. And she knew why her stomach felt so queasy.

"You're leaving honey," her Aunt told her. "It's the only way. I've made arrangements for you to take the train to Atlanta."

Anna's throat knotted. She stared at her Aunt's back, which was stooped, as she slowly folded the clothes, careful not to turn around.

"Anna, if your father finds us, he'll kill you. You see, one more precious thing has been taken from him, and he just can't take anymore. I know him. That's why I'm sending you away. Your Uncle Mayo will meet you in Atlanta and from there he'll take you to Miss Chadwick's Orphan Home for Girls. They'll take good care of you there, and you'll get lots of learning. You're so young to have gone through so much, and I can't give you any more. You'll be happy there, Anna."

It was quiet. Quiet and suddenly cold, like someone had passed. Anna went and sat on the back porch of the old house, but she did not cry. She wasn't even mad. For in the few short years that she had lived, she just figured this is how things were going to be—always. Anna watched as old Ben loaded her things onto the wagon. She got up and sat beside her Aunt and the horses took off. No words were spoken. There really wasn't much to say, and soon the depot was in view.

They dismounted and sat on the benches but still were silent. Every now and then Aunt Nancy would dab at her eyes, and Anna reassured her by laying her head on her shoulder. Soon the train screeched to a halt, and people were getting both on and off, walking quickly, shoving, and grabbing at luggage. Anna looked at her Aunt Nancy and they walked to the platform. She listened quietly as the porter was told to look after her and see to it that she got off in Atlanta. The conductor yelled, "All aboard!"

Grabbing Anna to her, Nancy held her tightly, closely, in a way that Anna knew meant good-by. The tears came from them both as they cried.

"I love you Aunt Nancy, I love you. And I know that besides Momma and the children, you're the only one to really love me."

Then the porter took her hand, and led her to her seat, as the train slowly pulled off and Aunt Nancy became as everything else—small, distant, and only a memory.

The train moved slowly at first, puffing and scooting, almost like a toy along the tracks. Through teary eyes and the window, Anna watched all that she had known and become accustomed to fade. Cheese's grocery store came and went. Funny, it didn't seem so big now. Everything whipped by, faster and faster until everything blurred into a colored streak. Then Anna settled back in her seat—the day, the past, Atlanta—whirling in her mind. She pulled her coat tighter around her and laid her head on the arm of the chair. The porter came by with a smile and a blanket and covered her. Snuggling beneath it, she covered her head and cried, never feeling more alone in her life. She was six years old and felt forty-six. She was tired, and soon she slept, not waking until the train creaked to a stop in Atlanta.

The porter woke her up and smiled as she neatly folded the blanket. Taking her hand, he led her to the depot where stiff benches sat in rows. It kinda reminded Anna of the courtroom.

"You sit right here now," he told her, his brown face lined, but pleasant. "Your Aunt said that your Uncle Mayo will pick you up here and take you on to the orphanage. Just wait right here now, he'll be on directly."

Anna managed a smile as he patted her head and walked away, then settled back against the bench to wait. She looked in all the faces of the men in the station, but if they looked back, it was only in passing. She figured he must be black because he was on Aunt Nancy's side, but no one stopped, not a black face, not a white face—no one.

Time passed—hours, and still no one came. Finally reaching in her brown paper bag, Anna began to eat the lunch her Aunt had prepared for her. She ate slowly, but only partly. Then, careful to save part of her meal, she wrapped it back up—her eyes saddening at the sight of Aunt Nancy's biscuits.

More time passed. The depot was almost empty now, no Uncle Mayo, and panic and desertion were starting to set in. She realized she knew no one. She didn't even know where she was going. But childlike logic and a prayer assured her things would be all right.

After a bit, a man walked up and sat down a ways on the bench. He read a newspaper, while sipping on a cup of coffee, as Anna watched him from the corner of her eye. "Is this him?" she wondered, but before she could turn he saw her and smiled.

"Hi," he said, and Anna answered, "Hi."

Then he went back to his newspaper.

A little time passed and the man put his paper down, stood up to leave, but stopped by Anna first, holding out his large hand.

"My name is Mr. Jackson," he said, "Mr. Charles Jackson. I just got off work a bit ago, and stopped in the depot to read the paper and drink some coffee. Little girl, where are you going? You seem to have been sitting for quite a while."

Anna shook his hand.

"I'm Anna," she said. "I'm waiting for my Uncle Mayo. He was suppose to meet me here and take me to Miss Chadwick's Orphans Home for Girls, but he didn't come. He's not coming."

The man sat down, his handsome, smooth face filled with sadness.

"I'll take you, Anna," he said. And he did.

Taking her hand, Anna and Mr. Jackson walked through the depot and down the way until they came to a worn streetcar that had just pulled up.

"You'll be there directly, Anna," he said, and Anna smiled. He was so kind, this man she did not know, and she felt like the little girl that she was, as she stood there holding his hand.

As he talked to the delivery fella who had walked up, Anna looked up at him. He was so big, so handsome, with light olive skin, and wavy hair. A thin moustache formed above a small mouth with perfect teeth and he had muscles. And he was so nice. She knew he cared whether or not she got to the orphanage safely. She relaxed, feeling safe as they boarded the streetcar and settled in their seats.

Along the way, Mr. Jackson talked a lot about his family, and Anna listened as she ate the rest of her lunch. He told her of his wife Johnnie, and his children, his youngest being about Anna's age. He told her how he'd done a lot of boxing, and how prejudice and politics had played a big part in his not getting his just desserts. He told her of his small house and the fence and flowers and swing that hung from the oak out back, and Anna's mind pictured and absorbed all she was told.

"Yep," he finished, "Johnnie is a great woman. She's pretty and quiet, but so wise. And cook! I can almost smell what's waiting at home. But enough about me, tell me about Anna."

She was quiet for a while, then started slowly. "There's not much to tell," she said. "I have two brothers and a sister. I'm not sure where they are right now. And I have an Aunt Nancy," she smiled, then told him about the incident at Cheese's store. He laughed with her and, all too soon, the streetcar stopped.

"We're here," he told her. "Let me grab your things and I'll walk you up. It's just around the bend a bit."

Mr. Jackson took Anna's hand and they walked together down the street. Then she saw what was to be her home. It looked like three Army barracks joined together, but everything was neat, and the grounds were clean and grassy. He knocked on one of the doors and was met by a woman Anna was soon to know as Miss Sadie.

"This is Anna Buchanan," he said to the woman. "Believe she's expected here?"

"She's both expected and welcome," the robust woman replied, as she spoke and carted off Anna's luggage in one breath.

Then Mr. Jackson turned to Anna, bending on one knee, looking into her eyes.

"Have a good life, Anna," he told her. "Somehow in my heart I know you will." And the friends said good-by as Miss Sadie returned to check her in. Anna walked beside her in the long hallway, a little afraid now, and wishing in her heart that the stranger she'd just met was her father and the family he was so eager to get back to was hers.

They sat in a small office and Anna was asked a number of questions, telling all that was deemed necessary. Miss Sadie in turn told Anna about Miss Chadwick and the Orphanage.

"Know what?" she told Anna. "Me and my two sisters Tugar and Bessie were brought up right here, and when we were grown we stayed on to help. This is our life, and Miss Chadwick has been very fair. You'll meet her soon. She's from England, you know. Word has it, her family's real rich out there, but Miss Chadwick figured she needed to do more with her life than just sit around drinking tea. So she came to America, her only purpose to start a school and help poor motherless black children—and she has. All her life she's dedicated to us and, believe me, sometimes people have tried to stop her along the way. Then we have Miss Fenicle. Now, she looks after the older girls, and is in charge of the laundry and teaching them washing and ironing. They're even taught how to make their own clothes. Everybody has a purpose, a duty, as we have eighty-five girls here. But I'll let Miss Chadwick tell you all about that. Any questions?"

Anna shook her head, "This place has so much order," she thought as she watched Miss Sadie leave the room.

Soon she returned with a tall slim white woman, who smiled and sat behind the desk. Her hair was neatly pulled in a bun at her neck, held by pins that showed, but her eyes were kind. "I've seen those eyes before," Anna thought." "Somewhere I've seen those eyes."

"So you're Anna," the woman said, her accent obvious. "Anna Buchanan. Your aunt wrote us a lengthy letter about you. I know your life hasn't been easy, and I won't promise it will be too easy here. There's a lot to be done, and we all work very hard. Besides, anything that comes too easy, really can't be very good, now can it? But I can promise you this. I know that, one day, in your heart, you will call this place home."

Miss Chadwick continued, "Now, let me tell you a little about us, before we give you a quick tour. Miss Sadie, Tugar, Bessie and Miss Fenicle are the very backbone of this orphanage. I must say I wouldn't do very well without them. They make sure the girls' rooms and dormitories are clean. Each of the older girls takes care of her own room. The girls in the dormitories are responsible for their own space, and they rotate turns cleaning the dorm. The older girls clean up the dorms where the smaller girls sleep, as generally they're not as tidy," she winked. Anna smiled. "But I don't feel we'll have that problem with you," and Anna winked and smiled back.

"Now, Miss Sadie here is in charge of the kitchen and with the help of assigned girls, she prepares all of the meals. There is also a dining room assignment, where the tables must be set and the food served. A bell rings for breakfast, but before you eat you must be cleaned up, your bed made, and at least your chores started. A bell will ring for breakfast, lunch and dinner, and no meal is started without first saying the blessing. Every girl also has an assigned seat at the table. If your duty is the laundry room, you'll be working with Miss Fenicle. We have a huge washer and each girl on this job has a basket of clothes to iron. The irons are heated on the stove, as we only have a couple of electric ones— not nearly enough to go around. After the breakfast bell, your chores are finished. Then in the summer or on the weekends it's off to the chapel. During the school year, of course, you must attend classes. Tugar and Bessie teach the kindergarten class, and the other children go across the street to Spellman Seminary. This is for grades one all the way through high school and college, and you'll be given a classroom, dormitory, and work assignment later. But first, I want you to have a chance to settle in, to feel comfortable."

Anna sat there staring at the woman whose graying hair fell awkwardly out of place at the sides.

"Yes, ma'am," she answered, hoping inside that she would be able to fit into so rigorous a routine.

Miss Chadwick leaned forward. "Anna, I know that this seems like an awful lot for a little girl to remember, and I really don't expect you to, all at once. But believe me dear, it will fall into place. It's funny, but I have a feeling you're a very different child, Anna. You're special—wise, but remember you're still a little girl, and you should never in life have had to worry so much. Now, it's almost dinnertime. Let me give you a quick tour, then we'll go to the dining room, where you'll meet the other girls. I have a feeling we have something that you'll like." With that she got up from her desk.

Anna stood up too, and they walked down a large clean hallway, where Miss Chadwick pointed out various things.

"We'll give you a better look at the place tomorrow," she told Anna. "I was a bit worried with you being so small, about you riding that train all by yourself. You're a pretty brave little girl, aren't you?"

Anna looked up at her and told her about the kind Mr. Jackson who had brought her safely here.

"Ah yes," replied Miss Chadwick with a smile. "The Lord has a lot of guardian angels watching over us out there." And then they turned the corner to the dinning room.

Soon they faced two big doors, and Anna could hear chatter beyond them. Miss Chadwick opened them and they walked in, the girls coming to immediate attention. Anna looked around. Eyes met.

"Everyone, this is Anna Buchanan," and a high squeal pierced the silence. It was Essie. She'd found Essie, and Miss Chadwick laughed as the sisters ran to embrace each other.

She'd found Essie, and Anna was happier than she'd been in quite a while. After a bit, Miss Chadwick restored order, and the girls sat in their assigned seats, with Anna conveniently seated across from Essie. At once the girls bowed their heads and started their blessing, and Anna, with her head bowed, hung onto every word knowing she must try to absorb them. So she listened intently as they all chanted:

Father, we thank thee for the night, and for the pleasant morning light. For rest and food and loving care, and all that makes the day so fair. Help the things that we should, to be to others—kind and good. In all our work and in all our play, to grow more like thee every day. Amen.

Dinner was silly. Neither Essie nor Anna ate much, for they were too busy grinning. Miss Chadwick sat quietly at the head of the table, indulging the girls somewhat, but still silently demanding decorum.

Soon dinner was over, and the older girls, when told, stood up and started clearing the table. The younger girls carried their water glasses and silverware to the big kitchen, and Anna followed suit. This done, they followed Miss Chadwick to the large drawing room where Anna was introduced to the girls who crowded around her asking questions. Soon they were joined by the older girls and Anna and Essie had a short time, after moving to a corner of the room, to reminisce. Essie asked about her Aunt Nancy, how she was, where she was. She asked about Doc and Roosevelt. She asked about Papa. She wondered if little Carrie still had sores. They laughed, and Anna told her that Aunt Nancy was getting too weak to care for her. She told her about the trial, and how afterwards she and Aunt Nancy had to run and move around so. Essie's eyes were sad as she listened to her little sister talk. She seemed so old for six years, so knowing. Essie was ten, but she, too, knew that life had been far more than one should have to bear. She decided not to tell Anna all that had happened to her since she'd been gone. That could come later. But what about Doc and Roosevelt? Anna told her she had not seen them since the day they'd run away.

 Miss Chadwick came in and told the girls it was bedtime. The two sisters said good night and went their separate ways—Essie with the older girls and Anna with the younger.

 She was taken to a large room with beds lined side by side, each identical to the other. Fresh linen and white blankets lined each, and Anna was escorted to the end bed by the window. The girls put on their flannel gowns, all made the same in the sewing room, said their prayers and climbed into bed.

The moonlight shone clearly through the faded shade, and Anna watched it, snuggling deep into the covers, until her eyes felt heavy. "Thank you Jesus," she half said to herself. "Thank you for finding Essie, and for the kind man who brought me here. Thank you for Miss Chadwick, this place and this clean bed. And thank you for Aunt Nancy."

The next morning all of the girls scampered up, made their beds and walked down the hall to the spacious bathroom. Anna followed everyone else's lead and soon stood in a huge wash room lined with bath stalls, toilets and basins.

Running to an empty stall, she turned on the faucet to the tub, and watched as the water streamed down, like an ever so small waterfall. She jumped in grabbing the huge bar of lye soap and lathered everything—even her hair. She splashed, letting the hot water rinse away the bubbles, never noticing that the other girls were out of their tubs and getting dressed.

A small girl named Catherine stopped by Anna's tub and told her,

"You better hurry, it's almost time for the breakfast bell."

" Breakfast bell?" Anna thought, but hurried to dry off and get dressed, dropping her night clothes in the large basket by the door.

In the hallway Anna noticed the older girls milling about and figured they must have been up before them.

Spotting Essie, she ran to her and was promptly corralled into another room with some of the other girls. Essie introduced her to her best friends, Trixie and Dolly, who in turned introduced her to their smaller sisters, Eva and Catherine.

"This is something," Essie beamed. "Now I have my own little sister to tend to." And with that Essie grabbed a near-by brush and started brushing Anna's hair vigorously. The other older girls followed suit, each checking the younger girl's hair and clothes. Anna was to learn that it was the older sisters' responsibility to see that their siblings were both groomed and dressed properly. She thought it was silly, but not wanting to be the odd girl out, she complied with Essie, who braided her auburn braids far too tight.

The bell soon rang for breakfast and all the girls rushed to the dining room and to their assigned seats. Anna was instructed to hers, not far from Essie—they all sat down knowing not to touch the food until blessings were said. They started together, all eighty-five girls and matrons, from all of the tables, singing:

All good things around us, are sent from heaven above. So thank the Lord, Oh thank the Lord for all his love.

Breakfast was Post Toasties or Shredded Wheat, with milk and orange slices, which the girls quickly devoured. After they'd eaten, the table was quickly cleared and the girls hurried to finish their assigned chores. Anna went with the younger girls and did all she was told until another bell rang; then she was instructed to go the chapel.

The girls entered the wood brown chapel, and Anna noticed the pictures of Jesus on the wall. She looked at the small hymn books, and the cross, under which was written, "Where will you spend Eternity?"

Settling in a pew up front, Anna listened as Tugar softly played the organ and Miss Chadwick started to speak. Anna hung on to every word, her small mind absorbing the messages from Jesus that would stay with her for a lifetime.

All too soon, church was over, and the girls were allowed recreation time outside. The yard was a huge fenced area with a number of swings, slides, and other children's games. Anna stood by the door, that ever present fear of unacceptance engulfing her. No one moved to her, and she was unsure as just what to do.

Spotting Essie off to the side with Trixie and Dolly, she walked over, and stood far too long before she was noticed.

"So this is little Anna," spoke up Trixie with a smile. "She is sure small for her age."

"And all those freckles," piped Dolly. "Where'd they come from?" The girls giggled. Essie giggled too. Anna just looked at them. Soon they stopped.

"Not too friendly, is she?" said Trixie.

But Essie quickly responded with, "She's all right, she's just new here and needs to learn the rules."

"Tell you what Anna, why don't you go play with Catherine and Eva?" Anna understood, and walked over to the younger girls. Sitting in dirt she watched, still hesitant to become a part, until Essie tapped her on the shoulder.

"Listen," she said bending beside her. Here at the orphanage the older girls are, well, in charge of you younger girls. You haf'ta do what we say, and hanging around us is unheard of. I'm a big shot here, Anna, and the girls look up to me. So could you just kinda be like the others? For me?"

Anna looked at her sister, hard, then over to Trixie and Dolly.

"Sure," she said softly, as the bell rang and they went inside for their afternoon meal.

Lunch was peanut butter and syrup sandwiches, with milk and a side of grapes. It was basically quiet, as this was the rule at the table. Anna ate her sandwich thinking how orderly everything was here.

It felt comfortable, and she smiled at Essie across the table. "So I haf'ta to play little sister," she thought. Well it was a small price to pay for the calmness she felt inside. Essie winked at her.

With lunch completed, the children were allowed to go either to the small library to check out books, the gymnasium for exercise or ball, or the sewing room—as long as they used their time constructively. Anna went to the sewing room and watched for quite a while as the girls made dresses, table cloths and frilly doilies under the watchful eyes of Miss Fenicle, who smiled at Anna as she caught her glance.

"Would you like to learn to sew someday?" she asked as she handed Anna a small, unfinished doily. Anna fingered the cloth, blinking. It reminded her so much of the doilies that Aunt Nancy had given her mother, and she held it to her, her eyes watering.

"Are you okay?" asked Miss Fenicle. "Anna, are you all right?"

Anna nodded yes.

"Would you like to keep the doily, and maybe someday we'll sit together and finish it?"

Anna nodded and answered, "Thank you," as she rushed out of the door. "Maybe I should go to the library," she thought as she blinked to keep from crying.

Pushing open a large door, which she thought was the book room, she was met with a loud "Shhhh!" And there was Essie, quietly sneaking the ginger bread cookies, as her two friends looked on, giggling.

"Be quiet!" she barked as she handed Anna a cookie and rushed passed her, out the door with her friends. Anna stood there, cookie in hand and fear in heart, as she quickly followed on the girls heels.

"I was looking for the library," she whispered.

"It's right over there," pointed Essie. "Now eat that cookie, fast!"

Anna ate the cookie and laughed to herself knowing Essie had not changed, as she watched the three girls scamper out the side door.

The library was filled with books of all kinds. Books of history, books of music, adventure, sewing and poetry. Black poetry and black poets that Anna never knew existed. She picked up one by Langston Hughes, reading a bit of his biography first, then settling back in her chair to read his *The*

Negro Speaks of Rivers, and the *Boogieman.* She was captured by his words, her young mind not always understanding them, but deep inside knowing of their power, for she had lived it.

While reading, far off in the distance she could hear the muffled strains of music—beautiful music, unlike her doodle-bug songs. And with the words of Langston in her heart, and the chords of the music in her mind, she got up, intending to find the sounds that had so enwrapped her.

At the far end of the hall, Anna pushed open a door to find Miss Chadwick cranking an odd machine that played music. She looked up, and smiled, saying, "Come on in Anna, do you like music? This one is called Roses of Piccardy. It's so beautiful, isn't it? Come on in and sit down. We have a few others." She complied as Miss Chadwick put on another record and cranked the machine like a person who had done this often. "Feel free to come into this room any time you wish," Miss Chadwick told her as she returned to her seat and introduced Anna to Beethoven, Bach, and Irvin Berlin.

The two were quiet for a while, then Miss Chadwick started to speak. She told Anna of England, and her childhood, which was so different from that of the little girl to whom she spoke. She told of her dream to help underprivileged black children, and of the obstacles along the way. Anna listened carefully as the kind woman told her of her many trips back to England and to different states, as she tried to raise the money to keep her school going. She told of the kind people she'd met, and of the rage and scorn she'd faced from those who did not understand.

"One day," she told Anna, "with the help from many kind people, I hope to build a new school. That's the mission I'm on now, and with the grace and help from God, it will be. You see Anna, my hope, my dream, is to cram as much love, knowledge, history, art and culture into every poor child that I find, for it is a hard, bitter world out there. For you people it will never be easy, there will always be a snag in the carpet. But if you can face it educated, proud and well spoken, you can easily surpass, or at least mend the tattered threads."

And Anna listened as the music played, and the wise words captured the small young child who was to live by them always.

There are other people with trials, she thought. There are other people who struggle, yet hit a brick wall, only to try again and again to succeed. But why? Anna wondered, as they both sat quietly in their chairs. Miss Chadwick didn't have to struggle. She came from a rich family, she was well learned, and she was white. Why would one woman give up so much to help her? And she realized that very day that she loved Miss Chadwick, for she was a combination of many people she'd known and loved in the past. Then, leaning forward, she touched the woman's hand and whispered, "Thank you."

She was answered with a warm smile, and Miss Chadwick pulled her chair closer. "I feel you're very special, Anna," she told her as they settled back to listen to a symphony with a number and no name. And the two sat until dinnertime, Anna listening to the music and the message, and every so often looking at the woman whose eyes seemed so familiar to her.

The days passed much in the same way at the orphanage, and Anna grew far more in knowledge than in stature. She remained quite small, but as Miss Fenicle often told her, she more than made up for it in brains, and just plain common sense.

And Essie? Well, Essie was Essie. She was smart enough, but the mischievous imp in her always kept her dangling on the edge of danger. She would fight or slap a girl at the drop of a hat, and more than once in Anna's defense. The girls found Anna both strange and withdrawn, and Essie had pounded more than one into the ground for their callous remarks.

Still, with all her defense of Anna, Essie still felt the need to dominate her, as the other older girls did their younger siblings. Anna took it in stride. She had far too much to do than to concentrate on Essie's whims. School was starting and her anticipation was high. Finally she could learn more about poets, other worlds and the composers with whom she'd grown so fascinated.

The first day of school the girls all stood in a line, breakfast over, their faces scrubbed, their uniforms crisp and starched. Kindergarten was taught right there at the orphanage, and grades one through twelve, plus college, were taught across the street at Spellman Seminary. Anna should have probably been in kindergarten, but because of her advanced knowledge, Miss Chadwick put her in second grade.

Anna found it a breeze—finally a school system that she could not be snatched from, finally a chance to learn and grow and read. Eva and Catherine were in her class and Anna was relieved. They were probably the only girls, besides Essie, who talked to her. All of the girls crowded to the front for the best seats, and Anna, with Eva and Catherine in tow, took a back seat.

"No need to cause a fuss on the first day," she reckoned as she sat at her wooden desk with the lift top. So concerned was she with arranging her pen, two pencils, and notebook, she never heard the teacher call her name. Then a tap on her shoulder caused her to look up to find all eyes on her, and the teacher at her side.

"Anna," she spoke firmly. "Miss Chadwick spoke to me earlier about you. She says you're very bright. Would you assist me in passing out the text books?"

"Yes, ma'am," she answered, and she followed the teacher to the head of the class amid the mutterings of some of the other children. As she quickly handed out the books, she was aware that this was another excuse for the girls not to like her. But she didn't care. Not right now. Sure, tonight when she was lying in bed thinkin', it would bother her. But not now. She was just too excited to finally be in school.

The teacher randomly queried the children, finding out what each knew or had retained. Anna did well in that. She did well in reading aloud. Then the teacher put math questions and an essay question on the board. Soon the bell rang for lunch and the children handed in their papers and raced to the lunchroom. After lunch they returned to their studies; then, before the end of the day bell, the teacher passed out homework sheets, stopping at Anna's desk.

"May I see you after class, Anna?" she asked with Anna nodding in agreement. The last twenty minutes were endless. "What could she possibly want?" Anna thought. "What have I done wrong now? Are they going to send me away?" The bell rang, and the girls slowly lined up, looking at Anna on the way out.

Staring at her desk, and fiddling with her pencil, she looked up as the teacher approached her, paper in hand.

"This is horrible, Anna," she started. "You missed almost every question in math. Didn't you understand the essay question?"

Anna was quiet for a while, studying the woman's face before answering.

"I guess," she said her voice low. "I guess I'm just not as smart as people think I am."

The teacher smoothed her hair and adjusted her collar.

"Don't worry," she said. "I realized you're new here and haven't quite received a fitting welcome. But remember, sometimes ready acceptance is not the best answer. Just relax and do your best. I'm sure you'll improve. You may go now."

Anna walked back across the street to her dorm. Her heart felt leaden, for she knew this was her last chance. She knew she must not fail. Walking past the other girls, she put her books on the bed and stared out the window. The autumn breeze slowly rocked the trees like Aunt Nancy's rocker, and she ignored the snickers she heard behind her. They only served to make her more determined.

This pattern went on for three weeks or so. Then on a Friday as Anna returned to her dormitory she found a note on her bed from Miss Chadwick. "See me immediately," it read. So again amid curious stares she walked past the others out the door and down the hall. Even from a few of the older girls there were remarks.

"Everybody thought she was so smart cause she's high yellow," mumbled one especially crispy dark girl. "Just look at her," commented another. "She sure thinks she's cute, and not big as a knitting needle." Anna kept walking. "Oh well," she thought. "Let them talk! But none of them better let Essie hear them talking."

Rounding the corner she knocked on Miss Chadwick's door, and received a prompt "Come in." Once inside she stood, not quite sure of what to do, but was instructed to take a seat and did so.

"How are you, Anna?" Miss Chadwick began. "Are things well with you?" Anna nodded. "Well, it's been brought to my attention by your teacher that you're not doing so well in school. Is it the courses, are they too hard? Is it the other girls? Are you ill?" Anna nodded no, her small mind straining for what to say.

"Anna," Miss Chadwick continued. "You realize that if things don't improve, we'll have to make some changes. I don't know what's happened but you must learn to speak up, talk to me. Why are you failing in school?" But Anna didn't speak up.

Changes, she thought. What kind of changes, what did this mean? Would they send her away? If she told the truth, would she be considered too big a burden? She knew she had only been there a few months. Was that too soon for requests?

"I'm waiting," said Miss Chadwick, her voice a bit more edged than before. "You know I don't demand much from you girls, but I do demand you be the best you can be. I'm still waiting. Anna," her voice continued, "do you hear me speaking to you?"

"Yes, ma'am." she softly answered.

"Then speak up," she was reprimanded. So she did.

"Miss Chadwick," she started. "I know I haven't done too well in school, but it isn't because I haven't tried. The problem is, I can't see. Everything on the board is just a blur to me. I didn't want to cause a fuss in class, so I just made do, and I guess I was reading the black board all wrong."

Miss Chadwick sat back in her chair with a small sigh.

"Is that all?" she asked. "You couldn't read the board? But why did you not speak up?"

"Because I thought if I did, the other girls would make more fun of me, and think I wanted special treatment. So I squinted my eyes real tight but it was still so hard to see. I didn't want to start a problem in school, so I just kept quiet."

"Now don't you worry," she was assured. "I'll take care of it. And, Anna, try to remember what I told you when you came. We don't live our lives just to please others—well, you know the rest. Now go wash up for dinner. You're excused."

Anna felt better already, somehow like when Aunt Nancy used to visit at her father's. She sailed through dinner, and rushed to her books, eager to prepare for Monday.

That Monday morning Anna went to school, as usual, with the other children. She sat in her seat in the back and waited for the class to start.

"Girls," the teacher started. "It has come to my attention that something must be solved before we start class today. Anna, would you come to the head of the class? Betsy, was it you who told me you had perfect vision? Fine.

Would you take Anna's place in the back, and Anna, you take this seat just in front of my desk." Betsy got up slowly, rolling her eyes at Anna as she passed her. But Anna took her seat, and as the teacher wrote a math problem in subtraction on the board, she answered it. For the numbers were clear.

This hurdle completed, class went on as usual, with Anna knowing the children would get over it. Her board work went up, her essay answers started making sense, and soon the classroom was back to normal. A few of the children even respected Anna's knowledge, for she found that after class some would gather and ask her questions. Not saying that she became popular or sought after, but at least recognizable for her mind, and thus deemed harmless.

The time, the months passed very quickly for Anna and the weekends were special at the home. There was so much to do. Every Friday after school, everyone rushed to eat and complete all their chores, for if all was done well, Saturday was reward day.

On Fridays before dark the girls ran in wild abandon about the grounds, swinging, see-sawing, or scooting down the long slide that emptied into one of the huge sand boxes at its base.

The older girls climbed the long ladders, or played baseball or basketball, declining the younger girls' participation except to fetch the balls. Anna usually picked the sandbox farthest away and quietly slipped into her dream world. Wetting the sand with a bucket of water, she would build castles and little villages of which she was the queen, the ruler, and the matriarch. Sometimes Catherine and Eva would join her, but more times than not, she played alone, for she knew their vim and energy far surpassed hers. They much preferred to tear through the yard with the other children. And Anna rather enjoyed these passive times when she built the small houses. It seemed like so long ago. So long ago when Doc, Roosevelt and Essie tore through the meadows, while she sat gathering sticks for her dreams.

A cool breeze and Essie's call rocked her back to reality as she noticed the girls gathered in the middle of the play ground to play *Hide and Seek.* They were screaming as Essie boldly proclaimed herself, *"IT."* The girls raced off in a thousand different directions, but Anna held back. She watched them all carefully, for she knew they'd be watching her, to find out her secret hiding place. She was never caught, she had the best hiding place on the grounds, so when they were almost all out of sight, she tipped off.

Running past the trees, the bushes, the obvious, she slipped behind the house and ran across the way until she reached an old shed that held the rakes and tools for the lawns. Then laying on her stomach, she squeezed beneath the porch that stood just inches off the ground. It wasn't roomy like the old porch, but Anna was a very small girl, and she'd lay there smiling to herself and playing with any bug that happened by. Sometimes, to herself, she'd sing her doodle-bug songs or her cucumber songs, knowing that Essie and the others were searching frantically for her. There was a smug satisfaction in knowing that if anyone should know where she was it should be Essie. For how many times had she dragged her from under the porch at the old place?

Pulling her sweater to her as best she could, Anna closed her eyes, absorbed in thought. There was her mother in her fantasy, her sweet face smiling, as she stood in the kitchen in a too big apron, her hair pulled back. She pictured her mother and siblings walking to the river with the loads of clothes and big bars of lye soap that caused her mother's hands to bleed so. She could see her smile, her eyes, and her slender fingers that could so gently braid her hair and touch her face. These had been such sweet times, such unsurpassable times that she would never forget. Then *He* would come home, sometimes calm at first, then the smell of rot gut would fill her nostrils. And then the cold harsh words came that transposed the smiles to tears.

Anna opened her eyes, and slid from beneath the porch, running as fast as she could to the big oak tree that served as home base. She didn't want to hide anymore, and she didn't care if she was *it*. Artfully dodging girls left and right, she knew it was time to leave the doodle-bugs alone, as Essie roughly slammed her in the back, screaming.

"You're It!" The other girls screamed their approval.

This Saturday, as every other, was abuzz with activity. This day became known as reward day or treat day, for good conduct and chores well done. Miss Fenicle and Tugar would hand out pennies, amounting to about ten cents, to the younger girls to buy peanuts and candy. On Saturdays a small stand was set up with rows of jars that held treats, and the girls took no time in racing to form a line to buy them. Candy sticks, salted nuts, and licorice faced them, and they bought carefully; for it had to last all week. Then, bags in hand, they would run out to play ball or skate, or just walk around Spellman Campus.

The older girls, as a reward, were privileged to go to a closely monitored movie, or swimming, or just have a nice trip out for breakfast. They loved this as it got them away from their siblings and also allowed them a quick peek at some of the boys. On Saturdays Essie always fixed her hair, real fine, for it was a taste of freedom that she relished. Once in a while, she would have to be detained at the home for something she'd done during the week, but she was usually slick enough to get away with most things.

Sundays were spent almost entirely in church and Anna found Sunday her most pleasing day. The words of the Bible she found fascinating, and hung on them like curtains from a too loose rod.

Miss Chadwick lived her life within those pages, and it was easy for Anna to see why she was so loved. Her proper words would fill the small chapel, spellbinding those who took the time to hear them, with stories of Jesus, Noah and Esther. She'd tell them of Jesus' life sacrifice, devotion and death for us, his children. She'd tell them of his love.

"For God is no decipher of man," she would say. "He loves us all—all shapes, all sizes, all colors. And he asks so little in return. Does it really take so much to serve him, when the reward is Heaven?" And Anna would sit there, her mind and heart racing—thinking, "I must do better, I must try harder, for my life has had no trials compared to his." Sometimes Anna would glance over at Essie, who sat in the corner, at times, giggling or whispering with her friends.

When she'd noticed Anna looking, she would stick out her tongue at her, and snicker with the other girls, and Anna wondered when she'd lost her. Yes, she was there, they were together, but more distant than they had ever been. When they were needy and their lives rocky, they'd been inseparable. Now when they had every chance to be close they were drifting apart. Sure, Anna understood Essie's need to be included, dominant, first. But at what cost? It was sad. She knew Essie loved her, but she was learning Essie loved herself and acceptance far better. It bothered Anna, it hurt her, but she allowed Essie to play her role, often taking her place as a compliant sister. Yet there were times, when they were alone, that Essie was Essie.

Another big day at the home was mail day, usually on Monday after school. Neither Essie or Anna got mail often, and when they did, it was always from Aunt Nancy. Her letters were long, sometimes rambling or repetitive, but always informative and Essie read them first, then passed them to Anna.

Anna always saved them until late, after dinner, because she liked to make them last, and liked to picture in her mind the words on the page.

This Monday, letter in hand, she made her way to the music room, for oddly this was the quietest place. The music seemed to soothe her as she read the words of the woman she loved so much. It also saddened her for, as contented as she was, she missed Aunt Nancy and the biscuits and the smell of rich chicory cooking on the stove in the too large kitchen.

Finding a chair in the corner, she noticed Miss Chadwick across the room, but pulled her chair closer to the window and opened the letter.

Dear Essie and Anna, I pray you girls are well, and miss me, like I miss you. I'm getting along pretty good, aching here and there, but as good as God's willing an old lady. I talked to Cheese the other day, he seems to be losing his hearing, but he said hi, and he sure wishes Doc and Roosevelt were around to help him in his store. Mrs. Taylor died a couple of weeks ago—do you recall her? She was ninety or so; anyway I tried to nurse her as best I could, but pneumonia had set in her lungs and she couldn't hold on. I don't expect Mr. Taylor will last much longer. He just wanders around since the wife's gone. Maybe I'll cook him some greens today and take them up.

You know, every time I go out back to feed those chickens, I laugh when I think of Anna eating that Chicken Feed. Do you eat it up there at the home? And Essie, have you calmed down any? You were always such a hard pill to swallow.

I heard tell from a neighbor that had been to St. Louis, that he ran into Doc and Roosevelt and they're fine. They used to drop a line or two, but I guess they're busy. Anyway they are still together, and I hear working in a store and fodder shop, but lately Doc's been seeing some gal. Isn't that a mess?

Your Pa is, well he just is. I think he's losing his mind. He's thin and mean as ever and drinking that stuff like there's no tomorrow. We stay away from each other, I've only seen him a couple of times, but word has it, he's got it out for me and Anna. That fool always did hate to lose. But he also knows, sure as death, I'll blow him away if I have to.

Miss Carrie is pitiful. All she just had to have, she's finding, isn't worth a grain of salt. She always looks beat up, and those kids—ugly as ever. That one still walks funny and the other one can't even grab grapes. Essie you'll always be a mess.

Are you girls happy? Are you learning? Learn well my dear children, cause you'll find this will be your measure in this world. Soak up learning and the words of the Lord and no one will ever be able to use you. Not for long anyway.

I've been doing a lot of searching, and asking a lot of questions, girls, about your mother. I think you should know, cause I want you to get on with your lives. I want you to look ahead. It's rumored that your mother, Lula died from that last beating from your father. Quite a few folks have told me that. A few others tell me she went mad, and was put in a hospital for the insane. Word has it she lost her mind, because she couldn't have her children. Now I don't know how true either of these stories are, but I know she's no where to be found. And I know that either way, she's gone from us now—so get on with your lives as best you can. No one ever said it would be fair. But I feel I made the right choice for you girls—a choice your mother would have made and I feel at rest knowing that now you have a small chance to make it in this world. So, do all you can to make us proud, and know I love you. Write soon.
Love Aunt Nancy

Anna sat staring at the letter, knowing that it confirmed a lot of what she'd known all along. But it's hard to let go of a dream. Sometimes dreams are all that keep you going. She needed someone to hug her. She needed her mother or Aunt Nancy to stretch reality and tell her everything was all right. Even Essie would do right now.

Looking around she noticed that Miss Chadwick had quietly tipped out and she sat in silence, the soft clickin' of the record player reminding her the song was sung. She left, walking the long hall to her dorm room, and laid on the small bed, the letter still in hand.

"Anna," she heard a voice. "Are you in there?" Essie walked over and sat on the edge of the bed, her voice lowered, as she knew she had no business in this dorm. "Did you read it?" she asked, not waiting for an answer. "Look, it's really what we've known all along isn't it? Didn't we always know that Momma wasn't coming back? Besides, we're still together, we have each other. Doc and Roosevelt are doing fine, and Aunt Nancy's okay. Papa? Well , he never was quite all there. But Anna, remember this, no matter how I act up here, I'm just showing out. You'll see, mark my words. One day we'll grow old together, and sit back and laugh at all this. You'll see. I gotta run now before Tugar catches me in here," and with that she was out of the door. And Anna laid there knowing tomorrow Essie would be Essie, but she, in turn, would feel a sadness for days to come.

Boy was she right. The very next day Essie was back to her usual antics that could crack Anna up so. How she wished that she could be more like her, bold and sassy, but learning only much later in life that it was merely a filmy camouflage. For Essie felt the pain too. She was just much, much better at hiding it, or maybe even forgetting it.

This week, as in many others, Miss Chadwick had a special weekend planned for the girls. They were all going on a picnic to Mr. Hendron's estate. Mr. Hendron was a rich black landowner who, throughout the years, would sponsor outings and financial support for the girls' home. And what outings they were. He lived on a country estate and always had large tables of food and treats to eat after games of tag and tetherball. They played with the small animals, and once even saw a pony's birth. The girls squealed. Some thought it was gross, awful, but not Anna, as she pushed past the others to get up front. She looked at the slippery, struggling animal starting life, and felt it was the most exciting thing she'd ever seen. She watched, her eyes never leaving the animal's, as the horse gently licked the little foal and she giggled as the other girls nudged each other in disbelief. Some of the girls didn't eat much that day as they sat around the tables, but Anna was non-stop. She stuffed herself, talking incessantly about the spectacle, to the girls' dismay. Finally Essie told her she was crazy, and a few others added she was weird, but Anna found she'd won a few supporters. Dolly admitted, ignoring Essie's glare, that it was pretty amazing, and Catherine added she though the pony was cute. Anna wished she could take it back to the home with her, and every time she visited Mr. Hendron's she would race to the stables or pasture to watch the pony.

Essie seemed to get more and more moody, and for some time had taken to ordering Anna about, even pushing or striking her on several occasions. Sometimes when she had candy or clean socks, Essie would just take them, exercising her authority over Anna as the other older girls did their siblings. Anna was totally unprepared for this, and she resented Essie's change of attitude towards her. She figured if she could treat her right in private, then she could treat her the same around others.

Eva and Catherine often cautioned Anna about talking back to Essie, but she'd grown tired of the abuse, and knew that sooner or later, it would come to a boil.

One cool morning as Eva, Catherine and Anna were walking down the upstairs hallway on their way to breakfast, Trixie, Dolly and Essie snuck behind them, walking on their heels. Anna could feel her cheeks burning as the younger trio was taunted, swatted with twigs, then pushed the length of the hallway. Still, they kept walking. Other girls gathered, pointing and laughing as Essie and her pals tormented their sisters, and their voices rung in Anna's head as they chanted down the hallway about her changing color.

"She's mean. Look how red her ears are! Look at her. She's mean!," the girls taunted, as Anna kept her stride.

When they reached the top of the stairs, Anna spun around, her books flying—fist clenched. Then grabbing Essie by the hair she punched her with everything that was pent inside, and the two girls rolled. They fought all over the hallway as the crowd followed, jeering and calling her names. And with every name called, "Mean," or "Red ears," Anna punched harder, the two fighting all the way down the bumpy flight of stairs— Bessie and Miss Sadie pulling them apart at the bottom.

"Did you see that?" the girls murmured. "Did you see her fight her older sister? She's mean, stay away from her, she's mean."

But Anna didn't care, for somehow this just felt too good for words, and she smirked looking back over her shoulder as the two were led to Miss Chadwick's office.

Miss Chadwick sat the girls in front of her and reprimanded them severely. "Blood sisters, and fighting like common enemies of the night," she scolded as Essie nonchalantly met her stare. Anna stared at her hands, her eye swollen, but Essie's haughtiness gone. "Aren't you ashamed of yourselves? What example are you setting for the other girls? For this you must be punished."

It was silent for a while then she continued. "As you know, this coming weekend is our last outing to Mr. Hendron's before winter. You two may not go. And every day for a week after school and dinner, you're to report directly to your rooms. Understand?" Both girls nodded. "I can't hear you!" she told them, and in unison they answered, "Yes, Ma'am."

With that, Essie was excused, and Anna looked at her just long enough to see that her lip was busted and her hair a mess. She loved it.

"Anna," Miss Chadwick continued, "this is so unlike you. What brought all this on? What happened?"

"I guess I just got tired, Miss Chadwick," Anna told her. "I never really meant to hurt my sister, it just happened."

"I know," the woman told her. "But you realize Essie's very popular here and this won't set too well with the other girls!"

"I know," Anna said, her voice not much above a whisper. "I know."

Essie and the others treated Anna like she had the plague for a while. And the day of the last big picnic, she stood in the window watching as the girls left.

"Well, busy yourself," she reasoned. "Write a letter or read a book." But this was small compensation. And she longed to once again see the little pony.

The kindling had to be cut every day, as it was cool enough now to start burning the coal and wood stoves. Different girls took turns at this task, as it was a rule that the kindling closet stayed full at all times.

Breakfast was usually oatmeal and Anna loved it. The girls who didn't would quickly switch bowls with her and she'd gladly eat theirs, sometimes eating up to three or four bowls, gaining weight along the way.

One chilly morning as the girls prepared for school, their oatmeal eaten or eaten by Anna, she noticed her pencil gone, so she raced back up stairs to get it. Some of the older girls were still bustling about, but she paid no attention as she looked frantically for the pencil she would not find. "It's getting late, better hurry," she thought, abandoning her search and racing down the emptied hall, the school bell on her mind. Anna was unprepared. Unprepared, as she was grabbed from behind and pulled into a darkened room. She struggled, but was bested, caught totally off-guard, as she found herself thrown in the dark, dirty kindling closet— Essie's laughter ringing in her ears. She heard the latch lock, as she beat on the walls of the closet. She heard the door slam behind Essie as the kindling wood dug into her arms and legs. It was dark, not a peep of light, and the coal that had settled on the bottom of the closet stung her nose. Pushing desperately against the door, Anna screamed out. Again and again she screamed, but everyone else was gone to school. Miss Chadwick, Sadie, and the others were downstairs either doing office work or washing clothes, or planning meals. She knew they could not hear her, but still she screamed. She was afraid. The darkness, loneliness, and silence were scary, like hiding in the back of Papa's wagon during a whiskey run. She pictured her father, eyes wild, chasing her, she pictured Miss Carrie. Every vile thing from the past loomed at her in that dark closet and the screams stopped. Then settling back against the panel wall of the closet, Anna began to sing her doodle-bug songs; the songs that had consoled her so often in the past.

    In class the teacher asked where Anna was, but the younger children did not know, and the other girls were playing possum in tune with Essie. Class time, recess, lunch, still no Anna and when the last bell rang, her teacher went to Miss Chadwick to inquire.

"Anna, not in school?" asked Miss Chadwick. "But you must be mistaken. I saw her myself right after breakfast this morning." And the search began.

Essie looked for her right along with the others with a smugness inside that she had triumphed. They looked right up until it was getting dark, and Miss Chadwick announced she was going to contact the proper authorities.

"Now let's prepare for evening," she said as she walked to her office, puzzled, unsure of how or why Anna would leave. And Anna crouched there all day, her body scratched and cramped, and her legs sore.

Now, preparing for the evening meant lighting the wood stoves, and the girls assigned to the task finally opened the closet, shrieking at what they found there.

"Miss Chadwick, Miss Fenicle, Miss Sadie, Tugar—come quick, we've found Anna. Hurry."

They all rushed to the scene, and Miss Chadwick gently lifted Anna out, careful of her bruises and cuts. The other girls gathered around to stare with Essie standing back by the door, watching her sister as she was asked, "Who did this to you? Who would do such a thing to you? Tugar, get some grits, bacon, and biscuits, and Anna, you can come with me to get your cuts dressed, and cleaned up."

Then Anna was scuttled out of the door, but not before looking at Essie, whose eyes, for once, looked wide and almost fearful.

The woman ran her a hot bath and Anna soaked, the water stinging the tiny cuts as she touched them.

"When you're finished," she was instructed, "put on your night clothes, and come to my office so I can rub alcohol on your wounds. Some of the bigger gashes may need a bandage or two. I'll have your dinner brought to my office. We'll talk there." And with that she was out the door, Anna's dirty clothes in hand.

Anna washed as best she could, dressed, and hurried to Miss Chadwick's office. Sitting in a chair pulled up to the desk, she said her blessing, and started to eat. The grits were swimming in butter and pepper and she dove into the crispy bacon and hot biscuits wondering if the other kids had had all this for dinner. The cool milk felt good going down, and for a minute she'd almost forgotten the stuffy kindling closet, but then the dreaded question came.

"Anna, who did this to you? I want an answer!" But none came. All that came to mind was the picture of Essie's eyes at the door. She knew Essie was walking a thin line here, and another incident might mean she'd be expelled. She may have to leave.

"Miss Chadwick," Anna started, "I was walking by and saw the door to the wood closet open, so I went to close it and dropped my pencil in. I guess I was leaning too far inside, with the ledge being kind of high and all, and I fell in. The door slammed and locked behind me, so I just crouched there and waited for someone to find me. Honest!"

The woman folded her hands and looked deeply into the child's eyes.

"Very well, Anna," she said. "Very well. You must be tired now, so if you're finished, you are excused to retire for the evening."

Anna, her cheeks somewhat flushed with the fabrication, rushed out the door and down the hall to her room. Her bed was a welcome sight as she nestled down, relieved to be lying down, but saddened by the lies she'd just told. Wearily she drifted off to sleep, not knowing if she was helping Essie or hurting her, and worse, not knowing if Miss Chadwick had bought any of her charade.

It was getting much cooler now and the wood stove burned most of the time. Things had settled down with Essie some, but she still was just Essie, and Anna was learning to accept it. Besides, everyone was busy preparing for their annual play, *Over the Rainbow*. The play was a big event for the girls' home, and everybody had a part or a song to sing. Anna went over her lines again and again. She had a good, big part, and this was one time she watched the clock at school, eager to get to rehearsal.

After dinner and chores, the girls gathered in the auditorium, Anna feeling important as she went over and over her lines. Crepe paper snapped in the background as the girls bustled about with decorations, while some made props, or sewed costumes. Money was tighter this year so they more or less had to make do. But nobody seemed to care, as they sang in unison choruses of *Over the Rainbow*: "Over the rainbow, over the golden strand, we're traveling hand in hand, over the rainbow, over the rainbow, right into fairy land."

For a month or so, everyone worked hard, especially Miss Chadwick. She made up hand-written invitations to all the surrounding donors and neighbors, hoping they would come to see how good the school was doing, for funds were getting so low. She knew after Christmas that, again, she must go to England, Boston, California, and other places to raise money to keep them going. But I'll worry about that later, she thought as she stuffed the envelopes, handing some of them to a few of the girls. Some they were to hand deliver, others were to be mailed, and the girls took to task, knowing play day was a few weeks away.

One more week to go, and almost everything was completed. Things were a little calmer now, but the excitement and anticipation were climbing. The girls loved it when visitors were coming to the home, for although this meant their absolute best behavior, it also meant a fine dinner and grape juice—with tarts and pies for dessert. Even Essie was always at her best with guests, for everyone knew what their presence could mean for the school.

A few days before the big event, Anna was feeling poorly. She was running a high fever and was put to bed by Tugar, who rubbed her with cool water and alcohol, against mild protests.

"Don't you worry none," she was assured. "You've just been working so hard, and you're not big as a minute. That's why you took so sick. You'll be fine tomorrow. Just rest." But the next day she wasn't fine. It was Saturday, and she woke up early, her head and skin hot from the fever. Her bones hurt, and she felt almost dizzy, but when the breakfast bell rang, she went. Picking at her oatmeal, she longed for the bell to ring so she could quietly slip into the music room. She figured if she could just avoid everyone all day, they wouldn't notice she was sick. She wanted, needed, desperately to be in that play.

The music room seemed cool as Anna sat in a far corner listening to quiet notes that seemed to amplify in her ears. But the music seemed small compensation for her burning, itchy skin, and she never noticed that Essie had quietly entered the room.

"Oh my Lord," Essie screamed. "You've got bumps and knots all over you!" Then runnin' for the door she yelled back, "You've got chicken pox!"

Anna pulled up her sleeves, and looked at her arms where tiny bumps were bursting up like heated popcorn kernels. "This can't be!" she thought, "This can't be! Not now, this isn't fair!" But it was happening and soon Miss Chadwick and Miss Fenicle had come and were leading her to a small room for inspection.

It was true. More bumps had seemed to pop out even as they walked. The small room was near the attic, and it was dark except for a small light that sat on the table beside the bed. "This must be the plague room," thought Anna, as she put on the flannel gown while the women went to the nurse. At the top of the room was one high window, whose panes were smeared with soot. A very light, misty rain was falling, beating far too loudly against the wood, and Anna looked about her. One bed, one table, one door, and one window. This was it. "Well, it's more than I've had in the past," she thought as she lay back on the pillow to await the trio.

Soon they were back and a stout, somewhat stern nurse started barking orders. "Run her a hot bath, and I'll need some baking soda," she told Miss Fenicle. "Miss Chadwick, she's to eat nothing but mush and soup, maybe a saltine or two. And liquids, lots of liquids. And you come with me." Anna did as she was told, and soon was submerged in a steamy bath. The nurse seemed to pour a bushel of baking soda in it, and then bathed her, quickly but gently. After the bath, she was rubbed with carbonated Vaseline, dressed and instructed to return to the room.

Miss Chadwick had sat a bowl of chicken soup, saltines, and milk on the table, which Anna started to eat. But she wasn't very hungry. She kept thinking about the play, plus the Vaseline made her nightgown sticky. Pushing away the bowl, she climbed into the stiff bed, just as the nurse entered, almost in a flurry. She watched as the woman skitted about tucking covers, fluffing pillows and moving chairs.

"Now," she said, "You are to stay in bed, eat as you're told, or at least more than you just did; and above all else, **DO NOT SCRATCH!** If you scratch those bumps, you'll be scarred for life. For the rest of your life!," she called back as the door slammed behind her.

Anna lay there in the dingy vacuum of a room and looked out the higher even dingier window. The rain made funny streaks on the glass and soon Anna's tears matched its pattern.

When the door opened and Miss Chadwick came in, Anna turned her face into the pillow, unwilling to expose her failing.

"Are you crying, Anna?" asked the woman softly. "Well you mustn't, for how often have I told you that life is not always fair? Anna, there will be other chances, there will be other times. And one day, in some way, you'll see that a star will shine just for you. It's funny, but with some people their rewards may not be on this earth. Now you rest. I'll sit here a bit, until you sleep." Anna curled up, feeling a little more safe, and somewhat loved. "There'll be other chances, other times," she thought as Miss Chadwick's low songs lulled her to sleep, like the songs of Aunt Nancy and yesterday.

The next morning Anna awoke, aware that the home was all a-bustle. This was the big day. The big dinner, the long awaited play. But the only bustle Anna had was the nurse bathing, rubbing and forbidding her to scratch.

And what a long day it was. The nurse seemed to have taken up permanent residence, pulling up a straight back chair, and reading in silence as Anna lay there. Miss Chadwick only had time to check in once, but she understood. This was a busy day. Meals had to be checked, guests had to be greeted, arrangements completed. So the time passed slowly, and Anna quietly lay there, thinking of all the *to-do* going on downstairs. She wished the nurse would leave for a while. Didn't Nurse Grayson ever have to go to the bathroom?

Finally she did, or at least went to do something, and as soon as she'd left, Anna pulled the wooden table over to the high window, to see what she could see.

There were buses, cars, and many people out front, coming and going. Some of the girls, stood in the cool wind, greeting, and giving instructions, and Anna took the end of her gown to wipe the window for a clearer view. She was absorbed with the goings-on, so much so, that she barely heard Nurse Grayson's creak on the stairs, as she returned to her healing mission. She jumped off the table, but too late, the nurse was already through the door.

"What on earth are you doing?", she screamed as she crossed the room, and pulled the table back into place. "Get back in bed!"

Anna dove into bed, more startled than afraid, and pulled the covers up to her chin. "Here's some books for you to read," she said a little softer, and returned to her perch—this time novel and knitting in hand. Anna knew this was going to be a long night.

Soon, no light was coming through the little window, so Anna picked up one of the books that lay on the foot of the bed. "Langston Hughes Book of Poetry." She, half-smiling, knew Miss Chadwick had sent them.

"*Over the Rainbow, over the Rainbow, over the Golden Strand.*" The words echoed in her mind. "*Over the Rainbow, over the Rainbow, right into Fairyland.*" And Anna turned to the wall, again burrowing her face in her pillow.

Funds were getting quite low and everyone at the school could feel the pinch. The play had brought in some money but times were so hard that corners still had to be cut everywhere. Miss Chadwick never gave up hope. Every day during one of the meals she talked excitedly about the new home she wanted to build for the girls. Every day she instilled in the girls the notion of hope and prayer.

Rumors were flying that unless there was a drastic change, or a miracle, some of the older girls would have to leave the home. Miss Chadwick spent many days and nights in her room praying, asking God for help—for people to open their hearts. And every time something ever so slight would happen that would strengthen her faith and clear her mind, she'd know it was all worthwhile. And there was always Mr. Hendron, who everybody knew was a God-send.

Then came the day that Anna remembered so well. They were released early from school and told to report to the library for a meeting. The library stayed warmer than the bigger rooms and often discussions were held there.

The girls were curious and fidgety as they waited for Miss Chadwick. Soon Essie had started a spit ball throw which ceased as soon as the big doors opened.

Their mentor faced the crowd and spoke, her voice as foreign, steady and soft as it always was, but Anna and some of the others knew something was wrong.

"Girls," she started, her eyes clear and scanning the room. "I've just received word Mr. Hendron passed away. I'm not sure just what happened but it was quite sudden. He did not suffer. Many times in the past he and I had discussed his wishes for this school, and he assured me we'd be well provided for when he died. But, as I said before, this was quite sudden and he had not prepared a will.

"As you all know, he was our most generous benefactor, but his estate has been mandated and we will receive no more money. I want you to know this will not stop us. I will fight until my dying breath for you.

We all know Mr. Hendron always wanted to help us. God only knows the hour of our death and if we don't legally prepare ourselves for dying, man or the courts can step in and diminish our life long dreams. Now girls, let this be a lesson learned. As we prepare ourselves for living, so must we prepare ourselves for dying. And out of love and gratitude for a very kind old man we've been asked to sing his favorite song at his funeral." And the room was silent—silent except for a few muffled cries and quiet prayer.

The funeral was beautiful, with crowds of people, white and black, who came to say their good-byes to the man who had helped so many. The girls sat in the back of the church—crying, listening to the organ, and to the tribute. Even Essie sat still. Soon it was their time to sing and they gathered around the casket, eyes filled, insides shaky, as they looked at the mahogany box that held their friend. Anna cried openly, remembering the pony and the old man's limp. But inside there was a small slight relief. He looked so calm, peaceful, and so at rest. The girls sang as the pipe organ hummed in the background: *When they ring those golden bells for you and me,* saying *good-byes* in a way they all knew he liked best.

Even though this was a set-back for the home, things went on. There were fewer treats, fewer privileges and more in-house work and activities. Miss Chadwick stressed the motto, *waste not, want not,* and everyone tightened their belt another notch. Breakfast had been reduced to a bowl of gooseberries, which almost everyone hated. Even Anna hated gooseberries.

One day at breakfast, after Miss Chadwick had left for town, Anna watched an odd activity at Essie's table. The girls were giggling and some of them were passing their bowls to Essie, who was bending down. Then the bowls came up empty. Anna tipped over, met by Essie's glare. "One word and I'll knock you into next week," she warned as the others snickered. Anna said nothing, just looked down at the hole in the boards. "So this is why they finished so quick," she thought. "They're pouring their berries in the hole." Then she walked back to her table and returned with her bowl, handing it to Essie who grinned as she poured the contents through the floor. Soon other girls had followed suit and breakfast was over. The girls took their bowls to the kitchen, and everyday that gooseberries were served, the girls giggled to themselves thinkin' of the fated gooseberry hole which was sure to be full by now.

But after a while the hole became second in their thoughts, as another Christmas was on the way. Snow covered the grounds like a picture hanging in old Mr. Hendron's parlor. Good clean snow that often served as ice cream when sugar and cream were available. The girls knew this would be a scarce Christmas but they didn't care much. It was just the season, the time, the feel.

One bright morning at breakfast they sat down, said grace, and prepared to eat their gooseberries—waiting for Miss Chadwick to leave. But she didn't. Instead she started to speak.

"I want you ladies, and yes some of you have become ladies, to know that I'm aware of your secret; I know about the gooseberry hole. I've known for some time." Her voice lowered as she continued. "I'm sorry this is all I had to offer. I'm sorry I've let you down." And with that she left her table. "You may continue your tradition," she finished, as she closed the door behind her.

The girls looked at each other, aware of the tears in Miss Chadwick's eyes. Anna swallowed hard, thinking, "She thinks she'd failed us. After all she's done, she thinks she's failed us. We let her down." With that, Anna grabbed her spoon and ate her gooseberries—spoon after horrible spoon. The rest of the girls following her lead. They never tasted worse.

When they finished, Anna took her bowl to the kitchen, and instead of getting ready to go to school she went to Miss Chadwick's office. Knocking softly, she was asked to come in and spoke right up.

"Miss Chadwick," she started. "I'm sorry. You see I put my berries in that hole too, not even thinking you were doing your best. It made the kids smile at me when I joined in. I never even thought about how it would hurt you. And all you ever think about is our well being. I'm sorry. I'm sorry for letting you down." She hugged the woman—both crying freely, both understanding that this was love.

Buon Natale!

This Christmas, unlike others in the past, was as expected. Even though a huge tree was brought in from out back, very little sat beneath it. Still, the girls took great delight in putting bright bulbs and stringing shiny tinsel throughout its large branches. This was always a fun time with everyone decorating the tree. They all sang carols, and somehow Miss Chadwick had managed to have a big pot of hot chocolate for them all. They relished it and Essie was quick to try to drink some of the younger girl's cups, but Anna was bigger now and she'd generally come to leave her alone.

Yes, the years had passed quickly and this new home had served Anna well. She'd learned culture, forgiveness and love, and even though Aunt Nancy's letters were few, she never hesitated to thank her for all she'd done.

The girls made most of their gifts to each other, wrapping them in plain brown paper. But *what's in a wrapping?* was the general tone, making do with what they had. School was on a two-week break, which in itself was wonderful, but two days before Christmas Eve, Miss Chadwick announced that Miss Sadie, Tugar and Bessie were to walk the girls into town—for they were all getting new shoes.

The air was cold but not biting, and the girls bundled up against the chill, eager to go into town.

They started out two by two, the older women in the lead, saying little but walking quickly. The girls chattered endlessly, quietly but non-stop, for town was always a big event for them.

Soon they were at the edge with tall buildings and shops in view. Stepping quieter now, like so many tin soldiers, they finally entered a large shop named *Prime Footwear*, and waited just inside the door while Miss Sadie talked to the proprietor. The girls stood still, aware they were garnering much attention but not quiet understanding why.

Anna watched as the other shoppers in the store crowded to the corners whispering, nodding their heads, their flowery bonnets shaking like wet bobbing apples.

"What's taking so long?" she wondered. "We only want to buy shoes." But soon she overheard Tugar say, "But we've money to pay," to which the response was, "I don't care if you brought the U.S. Mint here, I'm not selling any shoes to you colored's."

With that, the ladies gathered the children and started their walk back to the home—their step not so chipper this time. Essie was fuming and her comments more than made up for the ladies' silence. And even Anna, on this day, could somehow understand some of her father's rage.

At the door they were met by Miss Chadwick, who had watched them as they walked up the path. No words were spoken. None were needed as the woman quickly donned her coat and hat. And again they headed into town, this time with Miss Chadwick at the helm.

"There's something I must say to you," she said, her back straight, her stride steady. "I want you to know that I in no way condone this type of behavior, and I'm ashamed. Ashamed to call such people my own. But believe this ladies," she said, her voice rising. "You will all get brand new shoes on this day." Then she stopped walking and turned around to face the girls, who all seemed to stop in unison. Looking over the crowd she said nothing for a while. It was like she just wanted to really see them. Then she finally spoke. "Ladies, there is something I want you to remember. Throughout your life, even when I'm no longer with you, I want you to always hold your heads high. I will not tolerate anyone looking at the ground. Hold your heads high like the special people you are, for if you carry yourself proud, even though there's not a dime in your pocket, no one ever, ever, has to know. Now chins up, eyes ahead—we're going into town to buy some new shoes."

And they did. They marched with matched steps that seemed almost rehearsed, right up to the same store that had just refused them. "Mr. Jones," said Miss Chadwick, her eyes never leaving the steel blue ones. "I've come to buy my children some shoes."

It was quiet for a spell, as the other customers again retreated to their respective corners. The whispers welled up again, as all eyes, including the girls, looked into the face they all knew was no match for Miss Chadwick. For even though times were hard at the home, she was well known and respected, with a strength and pride few could put aside. Her name and her family's wealth were known throughout Georgia, and Anna realized that she and the other girls were witnessing first hand the moral that their mentor had just taught them.

The old man cleared his throat. "Very well," he said slowly, defeated. "Have them sit and I'll have my workers get their sizes."

And as the troupe walked back through the streets that dusk had darkened, they walked lighter, heads high. They didn't seem to mind the cold air as they marched, singing carols—a cardboard box of brand-new shoes under each arm. And dinner was especially good this night. There were biscuits and gravy with small bits of meat. Milk and small sugar cookies served as desert, and as all the girls went to bed that night they were overwhelmed by a sense of inner pride—pride in themselves, their teachings and especially in Miss Chadwick, who never ever seemed to let them down.

It was Christmas Eve. On this day and the next, almost all the rules were lax and Essie took full advantage of this. Breakfast and lunch seemed a waste of time to the girls, who only wanted the evening to come and the festivities to begin.

About two o'clock, the long awaited knock came and Mr. and Mrs. Cunningham bounded in with their dog

Queenie. They owned Cunningham Grocery, and every year at this time they brought over tons of nuts and candy to Miss Chadwick and the girls.

Everyone thanked them over and over, and Tugar and Bessie quickly took the treats into the kitchen so they could separate and dispense them in separate paper bags for each girl.

Miss Chadwick generally took this time to drink tea and chat with her friends, while the girls, who were always on their best behavior with company present, were allowed to pretty much do as they wished.

Earlier they had planned to meet in the music room to make sure all was okay with Miss Chadwick's gift. Since way last summer they had all pitched in to buy her a beautiful comforter for her bed, and as they spread the large blanket on the rug they examined it carefully to make sure it was perfect for the woman who had given so much.

Anna spoke up softly, knowing her opinion was not always welcome. It was Christmas Eve, and she figured everyone was a bit more indulgent.

"I wish we had a pretty box to put it in," she sighed.

"And I know just where one is," piped up Essie. "A couple of weeks ago I just happened to be in Miss Fenicle's room and I saw this big empty box pushed up against the wall. I'll just run and get it. Besides, she's having tea with Miss Chadwick and the others, and, well, she probably doesn't need it anyway." And before anyone could stop her she was out the door.

Soon she was back, grinning and lugging both the box and a sheet of red wrapping paper. "She probably won't need this either," she giggled as the girls, including Anna, set to the task.

At dinner there was a low murmur but still staunch manners, as this was always the norm at the table. No matter what day it was, Grace was always said, no elbows on the table, and no singing were allowed and using the proper utensils for the food must be used. But soon it was over and the girls were told to complete their chores, get on their nightclothes, and make sure all of their presents were under the tree. They moved like snicker flickers, eager to finish everything so they could sit around the tree for carols and treats.

Anna was the last to come down, as she'd been appointed to bring down the bright red package for Miss Chadwick. Miss Fenicle stood nearby, smiling as she watched Anna place the present beneath the branches. "She's so sweet," Anna thought, a bit guilty. "She knows we took her wrappings but she's still smiling." And Anna sat beside Essie, who laughed and talked as if nothing mattered. How she envied her for her ability to cope.

When all were seated, Miss Fenicle brought out a large bowl. Inside she had made her famous candied grapefruit rinds, sweet and sprinkled with sparkling sugar. Still smiling, she passed out some to each girl, never pausing at Anna, never acting like she'd noticed the package. This made Anna feel worse.

Soon, other treats were passed out—candies, oranges and nuts, and the carols were started. The girls milled about freely, singing and eating, and trying to guess what lay in store for them in the morning.

Anna was standing by the window looking out at the light snow that had started to fall when she felt a tap on her shoulder.

"They conned you into bringing down the package didn't they?" Miss Fenicle whispered, and they both laughed. This made Anna feel worlds better and she was glad she'd made her those very lacy doilies.

Again Anna stared out the window. She'd had quite a few Christmases at the home now. But still, a Christmas Eve that seemed so long ago stood out in her mind. And opening her bag of treats, she remembered the stocking her father had given her. She looked at the oranges and lemon drops, and that same overwhelming feeling of sadness engulfed her. She'd been so happy to get that stocking—she'd felt so special.

"Anna, bedtime," a voice broke in and she clutched the bag to her, heading for the stairs. "Don't dwell on things," she said over and over to herself as she lay in bed. "Anna, be happy it's over." But the thoughts still came of Mamma, Aunt Nancy, Doc, Roosevelt, and of a Christmas Eve so very long ago.

With the holidays over, things settled down to the usual, with Essie again up to her antics. Anna never could quite understand why she did things that only served to be her downfall, yet Essie was a good person, just so defiant and set in her ways. This particular time she'd come back late from a Saturday movie, but for some reason Miss Chadwick almost overlooked it, as this day, at dinner, she had a far greater announcement.

"Ladies," she started. "As you all know, I'm soliciting vigorously for funds in which to build a new school. So, for the next few months we will have special visitors, potential contributors, who will be visiting the home. Need I remind you about your best behavior?

"Now, after said visits, I will be leaving you to go to Suffolk, England, and other places to try to garner money and help for the new school. You will be left in the more than capable hands of the other matrons, and I'm sure you will comply with them, as you do me. You all know that we have long out-grown these old army barracks, and these facilities will no longer accommodate us. We need a bigger and better library, music room, and auditorium. We need a science lab, better irons and washers, more books. And with the help of many kind and generous people, these things can be obtained. They are all within our reach, for many, many hearts are good and open. There are some that really understand what I'm trying to do here, which brings me to our most important guest. Mr. John D. Rockefeller II will be paying us a visit. He wants to look over our school, and our programs, and ladies, I know in my heart, God has told me in my heart, that our new school is as good as built."

The girls screamed, and cheered, and dinner was an incessant ring of chatter. Anna sat back in her chair, happy and content, knowing Miss Chadwick was realizing her dream. For hadn't she always told them "if you really believe in something and put it in the hands of God, all things can come to you?" Anna was seeing that this was so.

In the next few weeks there was a steady stream of people at the home, walking, talking, asking, poking, but the girls handled all with poise and grace. Sometimes a curious onlooker would throw a quick history question at them, and Miss Chadwick beamed as they answered correctly and with perfect pronunciation. She knew they wouldn't let her down.

One especially quiet day, when some of the to-do had died down, Anna, Eva and Catherine went out on the porch to go over a lesson—when they were almost startled by a tall man walking up the walk of the entrance to Spellman. "It must be him," Anna thought, and she raced across the street, with the other two in pursuit. Running in front of him Anna stopped, breathless, looking at the kind eyes that seemed to smile at her.

"How are you, Mr. Rockefeller," she said, "I'm Anna."

Bending slightly, he took her hand and smiled. He answered, "Hello Anna. I'm very well, thank you, and yourself?"

"I'm fine, I think," she answered shyly, amid the greetings from Eva and Catherine. The three girls watched the gentleman enter Spellman. Anna knew she would always remember his kindness.

Inside, the girls tried to act normal, going about their general routine, careful not to gawk at Mr. Rockefeller and his inspections. Miss Chadwick, her manner and appearance impeccable, strode from room to room, explaining, showing the work that she was so proud of. There was a light lunch in the dining room before they all assembled in the assembly hall to hear Mr. Rockefeller speak. In the meantime, word had spread of the famous speaker's visit to the school, and people seemed to be coming from everywhere, craning to see him or hear him speak. Some entered the small assembly hall to sit with the students, others stood in the back, or to the sides, while others just stood outside, peeking in the windows, to hear his speech. And this was just as Miss Chadwick wanted it, for the more people that came, the more people became aware of their plight.

Anna sat up straight in her chair, hanging onto every word of the man who had stopped to smile at her. He talked of hopes, dreams and pride, and held his audience captive, like a mutineer pirate taking ship. The applause played on, as he thanked Miss Chadwick and the girls for their hospitality, then descended from the stage. Miss Chadwick stood amid the ceaseless clapping and walked with him down the aisle and out the door. The other visitors trailed behind, careful to give them proper lead. The girls remained seated, waiting to be dismissed, and chatted among themselves, obviously awe struck by this occasion, and all this attention. "He must be a strong, powerful man," Anna thought as she sat back in her chair, immersed in her own private world. "And he shook my hand," she thought smugly, a smile crossing her pretty, freckled face.

It was quite a few days before things settled down at the school, and soon the girls noticed Miss Chadwick ordering suitcases and writing lists and instructions and they knew that soon she would be leaving on her pilgrimage for funds. On the Saturday she was to leave, the girls gathered around her, saddened by her departure but aware that it was necessary. Even though she had gone on many trips for help, this one was all too important, as there'd been no word yet on the outcome of the new school.

"You all know what is expected of you," she said softly. "I love you, and I'll miss you."

The winter months were winding down now, and it was cool but not cold, and with appropriate sweaters or coats the girls could again, go outside.

Anna and Essie had grown up in the orphanage, and the gawkiness had changed to subtle pretty. Only Essie's wasn't subtle. She was a teen now, and quite pretty. Her skin had turned to olive and she pinned her straight black hair up now, to accentuate her slim face. Dark lashes framed her dark brown eyes, her nose was perfect, and her mouth was always in a pout. Essie was aware of what she looked like.

In town the boys stared at her and she looked back, while there where several scrimmages with *in-town girls*, who were jealous. She loved it. She knew she was meant to have this much attention. Sometimes boys would throw a bouquet of flowers over the fence to her, and she laughed at them as she tossed the petals in the air. Anna often wondered why Essie and her friends huddled and giggled so much, and she prayed that becoming a teenager would not render her so foolish. On the other hand, Anna was twelve now, and in the seventh grade. Although almost a teen, she still looked like a child. She was still very small, but her auburn hair was now brown, and the freckles were disappearing. She didn't turn olive, like Essie, she just stayed stark white, and she hated it.

Sometimes she'd stand in the mirror and pin up her hair, or try to look pouty, but she always felt ridiculous, and she figured she would never change. When someone told her her light eyes were pretty, she told them they were black. When they commented on her flawless skin, she thought it was milky. She felt she could not compare with Essie, who had always seemed to overwhelm her. Anna could not see in herself the things that others saw. But she knew she was smart, and so she settled with that as her calling. And Anna excelled in school, beating Essie year round in academics. But Essie just didn't seem to care, for she knew she had the look.

As the girls got older, the rules changed somewhat. No boys were allowed on the premises. Most of the girls would abide by this rule, but sometimes if they felt they weren't being watched, they would sneak and try to talk to some. The matrons realized that for growing girls this was a normal instinct, but rules were rules, and they had to be enforced.

Essie pretty much did as she wanted with Miss Chadwick away. She skipped classes, got caught in a few lies, and put some of her work off on the younger girls, who she seemed to delight in tormenting.

One day at dinner count at the table, Essie's chair was empty. Miss Sadie, Miss Fenicle and Tugar instructed the others to eat while they went to look for her, with Anna bringing up the rear.

They searched the house, the school, and then the grounds, where they found Essie, flowers in tow, standing by the back fence talking to a boy. Miss Fenicle cleared her throat.

"Miss Buchanan," she said dryly. "I believe your dinner is getting cold."

Anna shrank back. "Oh no! She's really done it this time," she thought, as Essie whizzed past them all, grinning.

Miss Chadwick wrote a few times to say her efforts were not going so awfully well, but was quick to mention that every little bit helped. She'd been gone a couple of months and was to return in late February or early March.

Springtime was aching to start early and the girls and matrons looked in great anticipation for her return. Since her leaving, some of the girls had again made use of the gooseberry hole, but finally it was announced that Miss Chadwick would be back the following day. Every girl took great pains to scrub and clean everything, and they'd even scrimped enough to buy some roasting hens for her arrival.

Everyone stood on the porch, but as the old car pulled up they could scarcely contain themselves as they dashed for her, surrounding her with hugs and chatter. Tugar and Miss Saddie pulled them back.

"Please, girls," they cautioned. "Miss Chadwick's bound to be tired from this long trip. Let's get inside first, before you maim her." But the woman just laughed. She'd missed them so.

Inside, as she sat in the dining room sipping tea, she called for all to come to her and, when they were all assembled, she started to speak.

"Ladies, you all know why I've been gone from you, but I must say that although we've received some monetary pledges, and offers of help with books, food, and a few essentials, we have not come close enough to build our new school. I'm sorry, but as we've always made do in the past, so we shall in the future."

The girls listened patiently as she told them about her many efforts. She told of how good it was to see her family again, and of the box load of new books that were on the way to Georgia. Also coming were a load of new uniforms, donated by a caring businesswoman, and from certain cities in the States had come offers of food, paper and pencils.

"So you see," Miss Chadwick continued, "even though we didn't get enough money for a new school, through the grace of God we have enough to keep us going for quite a while. Now I must tend to a few things and open my mail, so you ladies are excused." With that she turned to the pile of mail that lay on the table.

Sadie interrupted her with, "Maybe you should open this one first. It looks important." Picking up the tarnished silver letter opener, Miss Chadwick proceeded to open the long white envelope. It looked so official. It was from Mr. John D. Rockefeller II.

"Wait," she told the girls. "I think you all should hear this."

Dear Miss Chadwick: After our very pleasant visit, and much consideration, I have decided to honor your request for a new school. I, and my board members, feel that you are doing Georgia, as well as many under privileged children a huge service, and I will do all I can to see that your works continue. You may choose workmen, architects, and contractors of your choice, and we will meet to discuss your decisions in a week or two. Good Luck to you and yours.
Sincerely,
John D. Rockefeller II

Well, you would have thought it was the Fourth of July with all the noise. The girls and matrons screamed and yelled, hugging each other, and Miss Chadwick sat back in her chair, eyes teary, knowing that there is a God.

A few days down the line, when things had calmed a bit, Miss Chadwick and some of the other matrons sat in the library going over all the events that had transpired since she'd been gone. Things had gone pretty well, as she knew they would, but there were a few very necessary events that she knew she had to tend to. Listening quietly, she took several notes, then asked to be left alone, for she knew she had a decision to make that would not be easy. Then, with her heart heavy, she sent for Essie and Anna.

When both girls were seated, she brought out a faded manila envelope, and thumbing through some of the papers, she spoke. "Essie, I believe you know why you're here and Anna, I've asked you here to better understand the actions that I must take. You both know that I love you very much, but this school is good because of certain rules, and I'm afraid several of them have been broken lately. Anna, I've known you since you were a small child, and Essie, you've been here even longer. That's why you know you're wrong. Please understand that this is not easy for me, Essie, but I'm afraid I must expel you. For some time now I've been overlooking your antics, mostly for Anna's sake, but I can no longer continue this practice. It's just not fair to the others. I will be in touch by messenger to your Aunt Nancy today, to see if she can accommodate you. I'm sorry."

Anna dropped her head, and the tears came easily. Miss Chadwick turned to the window, a sense of failure within. Essie stood up and walked out of the room, never looking back.

A couple of days later, Aunt Nancy responded. She would pick up Essie the following Sunday. Essie acted mostly nonchalant but the week sped far too quickly for Anna. Sunday morning in the chapel she prayed long prayers for Essie's life and Essie's safety. Prayers to diminish the overwhelming sadness welled within her, for although she and Essie had become somewhat estranged these last few years, she knew Essie was all she had.

The two girls stood on the porch together, Essie having said the rest of her good-byes inside. Miss Chadwick stood in the window of her dainty office, hanky in tow, watching, as the others held back, knowing this was not their time. For really what else was there to say? And words were few even on the porch as Essie was determined to be Essie, while Anna picked nervously at a lilac bush beside the stairs. Then all too soon, an old black car pulled up and they could see the flowered bonnet they knew was their Aunt's. She stepped from the car and walked up the walk.

"How slow she walks," Anna thought as she watched the old woman she loved so. Then she ran down the porch steps to greet her, burying herself in the arms of her Aunt Nancy.

The woman held her long then reached for Essie, who graciously complied.

"My girls have gotten so big," she softly told them. "Why, you're almost grown now, and just look at Essie. They tell me you've been cuttin' up down here. Well, you know old Auntie will find a place for you." They stood a while longer in their moment.

The front screen opened and Miss Chadwick came out on the porch, dabbing at her eyes and waving goodbye.

"Thank you for taking such good care of my girls," Aunt Nancy told her.

"Oh no, the pleasure has been all mine. I only pray to God that I've done as good for them, and they love me half as much as they love you," answered Miss Chadwick.

Then the trio headed for the car. After a few steps, Essie dropped her bags and ran back to the porch. Hugging Miss Chadwick she told her, "I'll write you, and I promise I won't forget a thing that you taught me." Then she ran down the walk to the car, leaving her bags behind. Anna picked up the bags and proceeded, with Aunt Nancy to the car. She put the bags in the back seat on the floor by Essie, but Essie kept her back to her. Then as she was closing the door she whispered, " Anna, I think I'm gonna miss you. Besides, you were the only one here who could stand up to me. I love you." And Anna responded that she loved her too, as she closed the door, knowing her sister was crying tears she wanted no one to see.

Aunt Nancy cranked down her window and reached for Anna, gently fluffing her brown hair and staring in the eyes that had darkened somewhat through the years. Anna held her cheek to hers, not wanting to let go as Aunt Nancy whispered to her, "It seems like I'm always telling you good-bye." Then Essie touched her hand, ever so slightly.

"Run Anna, hurry, go in the house." So Anna ran up the walk, up the stairs, and through the house. She ran out back by the big trees, not wanting to look back at her loved ones leaving, as she had so often in the past. She sat down by a particular oak whose shredded bark served as a vent for her frustrations. She tore the bark and kicked the twigs and leaves—crying, hating, and knowing Anna was alone once again.

Things were starting to change rapidly at the home, and Anna knew she'd have to adjust to Essie's leaving just as she'd adjusted to a number of phases in her life.

Soon it was springtime in Georgia, and colors started to sprout, like a quickly turned kaleidoscope. Preparations were being made to tear down the old army-like barracks that housed them, and with that came another announcement. Many of the older girls, or any girl who had some family to go to, had to leave. Everyone else was going to be housed in Dorm Three until the new school was finished.

Miss Chadwick and Miss Fenicle took on the sad task of notifying the girls of who was to go, and then set about contacting family or relatives to house them. Everyday, the girls gathered at the bulletin board to see if their names were listed, often crying if theirs were posted. It was heartbreaking, but there was nothing else that could be done. There was just no more room for everyone.

Miss Chadwick took great pains to see that every home was suitable and capable, and reasoned that after having spent all their lives at the orphanage, surely they were eager to finally be with family. At least this is how she reconciled it in her heart.

Anna watched the board every day for a week, but found that she was not listed. Then Miss Chadwick informed her that she would be staying because her help and teaching were needed, plus she knew her Aunt Nancy already had her hands full with Essie.

The day that the other girls left, Anna again found herself in the back yard. It was not that she was that close to any of them. She was just so tired of saying good-bye.

Standing by the same tree that had served her so well in the past, she knelt to pick up a few leaves that were discarded and moist on the ground. She thought of all the ones she'd had to say good-by to; her Momma, Pappa, Aunt Nancy, Doc, Roosevelt, Essie. She thought of Cheese's grocery and of the doodle-bugs that seemed so long ago, and she thought of Miss Chadwick. Soon she heard the noise subside out front and figured all of the girls were gone, so she went inside, thankful she had said her good-byes the night before.

Inside, the mood was quiet and somber, as the remaining girls carried their belongings to Dorm III. Anna was already settled there, her bed pushed against the window, her things underneath.

The Dorm soon stood four rows deep with beds all crammed uncomfortably together like wooden matches in a box. By dinnertime, everyone was exhausted, yet relieved that they'd been too busy to think about the others leaving. They knew this would come much later, when they were alone in bed with their thoughts.

The next day there was school as usual, with the rest of the time set aside for completing all of the things left undone. Word had it that the men were coming to tear down Dorms I and Dorm II in a couple of weeks, so there was a lot to do. Before long all were settled in their cramped quarters, and none was the worse for wear.

Rumors spewed about that Dorm III was haunted, and often at night the girls would tell ghost stories in the dark. Sometimes Tugar would give them salted popcorn in paper bags and they would sit on the large round rug in the dorm, and tell their tales by the light of a kerosene lamp.

Needless to say they scampered nervously to bed and the lamp stayed on all night; everyone was too scared to blow it out. But everyone tried to make the best of things and get along; Miss Chadwick seemed so busy and absent the last couple of months.

Soon the girls were told that the demolition was to begin. Miss Chadwick had informed them that she had chosen all the workers, planners, and builders, and before long they began to arrive. The girls nudged each other, for they were all black. Black wreckers, black builders, black contractors, and even a black architect. Anna and the girls were so proud.

The men made quick work of the old Dorms. They seemed to go down so fast. That Saturday, there was no need for many chores, there wasn't that much to clean, so the girls had a good chance to watch. The dust billowed about the huge wrecking ball and Anna smiled to herself, thinking they reminded her of huge mechanical doodle-bugs.

Anna remembers one man in particular who always came to work in a neat business suit, his tie straight, his shoes shined. One day as she was coming downstairs, she was met by a rushing policeman who passed her on the way to Miss Chadwick's, so she paused to listen. Miss Chadwick came to the top of the stairs, and his surprise was noticeable as he fumbled with his words. I guess he just couldn't believe that a white woman ran a house for black children only.

Miss Chadwick faced him and asked, "What do you want?"

She was met with a short pause before he could speak.

"I have a man in my police car who says he works for you. I think you'd better come check this out." He turned to go back to his car.

Miss Chadwick followed and noticed her worker in the car, held by two other officers. One of them said, "Why, you're Miss Chadwick. I guess everybody around here has heard about you." But she did not respond, only looked at all three squarely as the lean one continued. "Now, he says he works for you on this new building here, but he doesn't look like he's coming to work all dressed up like he is. Besides where'd he get a suit and shoes like this?"

The woman smiled slightly before she spoke. "Gentleman," she started. "I can assure you that I do not know who his tailor is, but he does work for me. Now release him, so he can go about his work, and I can go about my job of getting all three of your names and badge numbers. I'll see you downtown." With that she and the worker turned and walked toward the building, leaving the three with slightly auburn cheeks.

Once inside, the worker thanked her, then went to change for work while Miss Chadwick pulled out the car to head for the police station.

Once there, she demanded that the three be harshly reprimanded, and that both the worker and the school receive an apology. She told the sergeant that this had happened several times, and she would not tolerate any of her team being harassed. And Miss Chadwick, being Miss Chadwick, got all that she asked for. Anna always marveled at the kind white woman who would put so much on the line for those not of her own blood.

And even though things were looking up, the new school was being built, and help was more plentiful than ever before, there were still many stumbling blocks that Miss Chadwick had to fight. And yes, she was despised by some whose narrow minds and evil hearts were as closed as sealed tombs. Still she fought on.

It was almost summer time now. School was out, and the girls had a lot to do with fewer girls to do it. New assignments were given. Anna and Catherine were to go to the neighborhood grocery to shop for anything missed by the big shopping, usually done by Miss Fenicle and Miss Sadie. The girls were excited to go alone that first time, holding tightly onto the money and the short list. It was important to them that they were chosen and so trusted.

As they entered the store, Anna grabbed a wooden basket and proceeded to case the aisle with Catherine right behind her, giggling at the Bunyan Pads and lice creams. Finally they got their four items and went to the counter to pay, where they were met by a rather fat man with a dirty apron, whose head was too small for his body.

"Excuse me sir,'" Anna spoke up. "We're from Miss Chadwick's girls' home and she sent us to pick up these few items."

Catherine handed him the money, which he snatched quickly like it was burning coals. Muttering aloud, he took his time figuring their items, hating to wait on them, yet not stupid enough to ignore their cash. Then he threw their change on the counter, folded his swelled arms, and stood back looking at the girls like an oversized Christmas bulb. Anna looked right back at him, and then said to Catherine, "Let's go." They headed for the door, leaving the change on the counter.

Catherine was shaking, more from anger than fear, as the girls walked the short distance back to the school, their bubble burst. But Anna told her, "I guess he figured if he handed the change, some of this color would rub off." She giggled, knowing there really wasn't much color on her to rub off.

When they reached the school, they told Miss Chadwick what had happened, and where the change was. With the two in tow, Miss Chadwick headed back to the store, where she crowded in line to confront the man about his actions.

It was funny how fools never really had much to say when Miss Chadwick faced them, and the girls smiled openly at the swollen man as the woman held out Anna's hand. He gently placed the change inside. For he knew that the school did a lot of trade with his store. He conceded, knowing that their buying filled the huge bulge around his waist. From then on there was never a problem when the girls shopped at the store. Oh, he may have hated them, but he respected them, and that was all they wanted in the first place.

But these problems were to continue, some bigger than others, some easily solved, some not. Like the one that warm night at dinner when Miss Chadwick told the girls of the death threats she'd been receiving. She told them the authorities were looking into it, but they thought it best that she leave for a while, and she instructed them to carry on as usual without her. The silence that fell told all, as the girls felt confused and angered that anyone could want to harm her.

Miss Chadwick went on to say that the person had stated they were coming to the home for their cowardly deed, and they even went so far as to state the day and the time. The girls were told to tell all strangers and even people they knew that she simply was not there, for it seemed some folks were angered because she'd used all black workers for the new building. She explained that what she'd viewed as a much needed first, others had seen quite differently, but she assured them that when all was well she would return.

That night, scattered, muffled cries could be heard throughout the dorm, for this was something that no one had ever anticipated, and some of the girls were realizing how unfair life could be.

Miss Chadwick left the next morning, quietly, unceremoniously, and as she put her bags in the shiny car, she told the girls that she would write and the matrons would relay all messages. Rolling down the windows, she waved at them all, saying she'd be back in two or three months.

"Just wait for that one letter," she told them as the car pulled off, leaving a string of dark smoke and broken hearts.

The time passed slowly, and each day the girls checked the mail for Miss Chadwick's return. Some girls got mail, but the letters from Essie to Anna had been few and far between. Generally Essie spoke of working and feeling free, and how Aunt Nancy really didn't understand her, with very little said about the home, except that she sometimes missed it.

Anna wrote back of the new building's progress and about Aunt Nancy. She asked if there was any word of Pa, and said that she missed them. Sometimes she wrote about the fight they'd had on the stairs to make Essie laugh, or she asked if there was any word on little Carrie and her burned thighs, or the sister with the stubby fingers.

One particular hot day as Anna sat out by the fence, Eva came to her saying there was a letter from Miss Chadwick, addressed to them all. She said Miss Fenicle had read it, and Miss Chadwick said all was well and she'd be home soon. She then handed her a rather plump letter from

Essie and ran back to the school, leaving Anna with her privacy to read.

Leaning back against the fence post, Anna thought about Miss Chadwick. She'd been gone almost two months now, and it would be good to have her home. "I hope she's getting her much needed rest," she thought as she tore open the letter from Essie. It read:

Dear Anna,

I know I haven't written like I should, but I've been keeping pretty busy. There's always a lot to do here with Aunt Nancy, and she's getting up in age now. There is a lady who stays with us a lot of the time and she's a real help. Her name is Vionette. That's kinda different isn't it? Anyway I've got a real job that I'll be starting in about a week, also it may be a long time before you hear from me again. But don't worry. I'll be fine. The job is with an Army Captain and his family, I'll be cooking and cleaning for them and taking care of their kids. I get room and board, and even pay for my work. His name is Captain Jenkins and both him and his wife are real nice. I'm not sure about the kids yet, as I haven't really spent much time with them, but I hope it will work out. I'm real excited about this job, and guess what? I get to travel all over with them, all over the country, wherever they go, I go. This should be a chance of a lifetime.

How's Miss Chadwick? It's funny but when Captain Jenkins wrote the school about me, she gave me a great reference. I kinda miss her, I guess she and Aunt Nancy always seem to come through for us in the long run, huh?

Have you heard anything about Trixie and Dolly? They both wrote me a couple of times, but we seem to have lost contact. I heard they were going to Colorado somewhere.

Aunt Nancy is doing pretty good. She doesn't see very well, and she has arthritis or something in her hands. Vionette takes real good care of her. As far as Pa is concerned, I heard he's still rantin' about getting folks, and drinking whiskey. I'm not sure if he's still with Miss Carrie or not, but I haven't heard anything about her kids. Not that I ever want to.

Doc and Roosevelt. Well, I guess we've seen the last of them. I wouldn't even know where to begin looking, and I'm sure they'd never be able to find either one of us. But the old lady who lives in the next county said she heard that one of them was married. She wasn't sure which one. Can you picture that?

Anna, I've heard a couple of things about Momma since I've been back. One is Papa killed her when he shot at her in the fields. The other is she lost her mind and was committed to an insane asylum because she couldn't have her kids. I'm not sure which is true, but do we really want to know? Maybe it's best we just remember her, as she was.

I know sometimes we didn't get along so well, and sometimes I acted like a fool, being obnoxious and trying to snatch the attention from you. But I really do care about you. I've always known I could never be as sweet or smart or quietly pretty as you, and I guess I've always been jealous, yes jealous because I could never possess all the things that you are. Well I'm gonna close for now. Take care of yourself Anna and know that I miss you. until we write again.

Love,
Essie

A lump was welling in Anna's throat as she read the letter again, trying desperately to hold on to that part of Essie that she could not help missing. She thought of her siblings all scattered about like seeds in a sudden gale, and she ached. For all she'd ever wanted was a stable home. She thought of the stories of long ago about other family members being sold in front of the store, and she identified with their feelings of utter hopelessness. She wondered if she'd ever see Essie or any of the others again.

Just then Catherine came bouncing across the yard, pigtails flying, interrupting Anna's solitude that she so needed at this time.

"Anna, come up to the house," she yelled. "Miss Chadwick's home. She got here the same day as her letter."

Anna snapped back to reality. Standing up she headed towards the house. She felt better; Miss Chadwick was home. "Yet it's funny," she thought, quickening her walk to a run. "With me, people are always either coming or going."

Finally the day came when the new building was completed, and what a relief it was. Even though it was fun at first with all the girls living in one dorm, after a while the cramped conditions were getting unbearable.

And what a difference it was from the old Army barracks. It had four entrances. Five, if you counted the basement entrance, in back, that led to the driveway and garage. The driveway was on an incline from the street, all cement and clean, and in it sat a brand new car, shining against the bright sun, like a rubbed new copper penny.

And oh, what a grand tour the girls had. The garage door led into a full finished basement, with a huge area for skating and other entertainment, and in the corner sat a large fireplace.

Further on, in the back of the basement, a door led to a trunk room, where most of the older girls could comfortably store their belongings, and to the left was the furnace room. A real furnace, and everybody knew what that meant. No more coal and wood stoves for their heat. No more chopping kindling in the cold.

In the back to the right was the new laundry room, with huge institutionalized washers and dryers. A few clotheslines hung at the rear, and adjacent to the laundry room there were several storage areas. These rooms held detergent, canned foods, shovels, Christmas decorations and anything else that had so cluttered the premises of the former building.

At the end of the basement stood an entrance that would lead upstairs. Beyond that door, between stairways, were two additional doors—one leading directly to the yard outside, the other inviting them to a long hallway on the first floor.

Here they encountered the kitchen, a large room with big new stoves, refrigerators, and cooking space. Cabinets and shelves lined the wall, stocked to the brim with the things that for so long they had done without.

The girls were amazed, and Anna stood in the kitchen looking around as if she was dreaming. What especially caught her eye was the shiny red and white broken tile, which gleamed up at her so clearly she saw her reflection. They all followed the tile to the panty area where they were met by more counters, shelves and even a few machines that they had never seen before. The girls learned that these were to help them with cutting food, or dicing, and one was a special machine designed to make mayonnaise.

The pantry led to the back porch, with a hanging bench swing to the right, and wooden chairs to the left, all lined up neatly on the same shiny red and white tile. Anna knew, as she again looked at her reflection, that she would spend many days on this porch reading, or just thinking of the things that meant so much to her.

Back through the kitchen and down a long hallway was the large dining room for the girls, with a big table sitting sternly in the center, but softened somewhat by the dainty bouquet of assorted flowers that sat haughtily on top.

Next was the Matrons dining room, somewhat smaller than the girls but elegant to them by any standards. Anna thought that from now on the girls would be eating all alone, and she grinned thinking of how Essie would have taken advantage of this situation.

Now they were escorted down a long hallway that ran the entire length of the building, with doors on each end leading to the outside porches. On one side of the hallway was a reception room where visitors or relatives could talk to the girls. Next to it was Miss Chadwick's office, proper and neat with a large oval rug in the center. Right off of it was a smaller office where the girls on office duty could work comfortably.

Further on was the Chapel, brilliantly adorned with stained glass and Jesus. Smooth wooden pews lined with spankin' new songbooks sat proudly facing the pulpit, which was introduced by a long red runner of new carpet.

The library was immense. Miss Chadwick explained the many companies and individuals who donated numerous new books. Anna ran to the shelves, fingering *The Tarzan and Elsie Dinsmore Series*. She thumbed through volumes of knowledge, history and cultured events, knowing surely that this was one of her favorite rooms. Except for the next one.

The music room, where beautiful pictures of scenes and famous composers lined the walls as if they were holding court. Racks of music stood all about, and a smaller shelf housed scores and sheet music for the girls to learn and enjoy. A piano and several new instruments and horns sat in one corner, and Anna thought to herself that even if none of the girls ever talked or played with her again, she could be happy here for the rest of her life.

Anna knew she'd never really been popular or accepted by the other children, but for some reason, today it did not matter, for Miss Chadwick and the other Matrons were quite fond of her, and she of them. She was their favorite, and to her this was really what mattered. Besides, in a wonderful new place like this, one could surely lose oneself within oneself—couldn't one? Yet as she watched the others, huddled together, giggling, poking, an inner part of her defied her sound reasoning and she was lonely. Even with all the gala festivities, she was alone.

The next stop was the second floor with the bedrooms, and a large room called the sleeping porch.

The older girls had smaller rooms, but were only two to a room. The next set, of which Anna was included, as she was about thirteen or so—housed four. These rooms were much larger and each girl had more than ample space, with the area by the window allotted to Anna.

The very young girls' quarters was a huge sleeping porch with wooden ducks and horses smiling from the walls with a child like innocence. Anna remembered how when she'd first come to the home, she would have been placed with them. And now in a year or so she'd be housed in the oldest girls' quarters—and she smiled at the little faces jumping about excitedly at their new gift. The little children were so dear to her.

Every room or dormitory had a sink and dressing area, and enough closet space for everything to be placed neatly. New spreads covered the beds, and the windows hosted new curtains with frilly trim that everyone knew Miss Fenicle had taken weeks to make.

Miss Chadwick's and Miss Fenicle's rooms were a short distance from the older girls rooms, and Miss Saddie, Tugar and Bessie had rooms off of the smaller girls' sleeping porch. Miss Fenicle and the other Matrons' quarters were roomy and decorated to their own specific needs and tastes, allowing each woman the space for her much earned privacy.

Miss Chadwick, much to the others' disdain, had tried to keep her room simple, but with much coercing and planning from the other matrons, it had turned out quite elaborate. The girls peered in the doorway at the huge bed, the sheer curtains, and the large oak dressing table with its carved design and huge mirror.

The girls thought it was beautiful, and they expressed it over and over, touching, giggling with excitement. Anna thought that this room was perfect, just like the woman, and she knew that Miss Chadwick was finally reaping some of what she'd sacrificed and worked so hard for.

But Miss Chadwick seemed a little embarrassed by their attention and she quickly ushered the girls down the hall to Miss Fenicle's new sewing room.

The second floor also had large bathrooms, bath areas, and dressing rooms, stocked with rolls of toilet paper and pink and green soap. The girls figured that surely nothing could be finer than this new building, and they intended to keep it this way.

The third floor was mostly for storage, with lots of extra space and two complete bedrooms, sparsely furnished with two small beds and dressers. Miss Chadwick explained that these were for anyone who was very ill and needed to be quarantined from the others for a while.

On their way down the long stairs to the main floor, the girls chattered excitedly about all that they'd just seen. Anna brought up the rear, listening closely as Miss

Chadwick explained that the rules were all the same, and each girl was responsible for her room, the smaller girls, and the chores as usual. And as Anna descended the stairs she couldn't help thinking that Essie would surely have loved all of this, for if home was just one definition, this was it.

Fall had seemed to come and go quickly and the girls were all looking forward to the holidays in the new home.

Things had been so busy this past summer that no one had really enjoyed their summer or autumn, but Halloween was just around the corner, and a lot of activities were planned.

With the building being new, the holidays somehow had a different meaning, and no one had to be urged to keep everything spotless. They were so proud of their new home they did their chores happily, automatically; the new red and white tiles always looked immaculate. With the new added conveniences, the workload had diminished greatly, so everyone was more than willing to always co-operate.

On Halloween the girls went to school, did their chores, and skipped dinner, as they knew there were a lot of treats around.

With all done, they went into the large basement where the matrons built a fire, a glowing fire that made their faces flicker and dance.

The girls were all instructed to sit on long benches against the wall and tuck one of their legs beneath them, with the other one hanging down. One of the girls would have on a fake leg, and another was chosen to go around to everyone and by pulling their leg try to find the fake one. This was not easy as all the girls wore long cotton stockings, and the bogus one was totally undetectable. When she came onto the bad leg, it would suddenly fall off with a clunk and all the girls would scream and run about, glad that she'd been caught, and they would get a turn. Next came ducking for apples in large vats filled with water. Each girl was allowed to keep two apples. Any extra apples were put aside for the girls who were not fortunate enough to nab one.

When it came to the game of picking up balls of cotton with a spoon from a large bowl, blindfolded, nobody fared too well. But the egg roll, where the girls rolled a hard-boiled egg across the floor with their noses, was Anna's sport. She won hands down, with some of the girls grumbling that she only won 'cause her nose was so long. But she didn't care. She got an extra bag of gumdrops for winning.

Next the girls put on their roller skates, skating round and around the basement, while the matrons put a huge kettle with wieners on the fire. Also potatoes with skins were put on the fire, making them crisp and brown.

After they had eaten, they were given bags of candy, instructed of their bedtime, and left alone to skate or just talk. But most of them were ready to retire, thankful that the next day was Saturday.

Anna sat in front of the fire looking at its colors, watching it perform, smiling, thinking, "I wonder how many girls Essie would have tripped with her skates".

Thanksgiving was always a festive but quiet day. In the afternoon after chores, everyone gathered in the chapel for devotion, and each girl was asked to stand and thank God for all He that had given them.

Anna sat quietly, listening, as Miss Chadwick, thanked the Lord for them. She smiled and her voice was steady as she gave thanks for having the best and most loyal family anyone could ever ask for. She thanked God for the new building, built by the generosity of others, and for keeping an ever-present watch over the health and well being of the children. Her thanks progressed to prayer and soon they were in a mini-church service, with others joining in to thank the Lord.

Then one by one the others stood to praise Him, and Anna closed her eyes, hearing stories that were so very similar to hers.

Soon it was her turn, and she stood, a bit nervous but overwhelmed by a feeling of love, focusing her eyes on Miss Chadwick. She started to speak softly, but confidently and truthfully.

"I've been here a long time," she started. "It seems like almost all my life. Yet, I have another life, a life that seems so long ago. I'd like to thank God for my Mother, my Aunt Nancy, my brothers, Doc and Roosevelt, and yes, for Essie," she said, smiling around at the other girls." I want to thank him for this new home, and for even the old building, for I've grown so much and learned so much from both. The things, and the love I've learned here I know will stay with me forever. God bless the matrons and teachers who serve us so unselfishly, and all the girls for putting up with my sometimes different behavior. And I want God to especially bless you, Miss Chadwick, for loving us with no thought of yourself, for giving us a chance to know about arts and culture, and things we may have missed if we hadn't known you. I know within my heart, that without you, there would probably be no me."

She then sat down, still nervous, wondering if she'd said too much, or sounded too white, or just made a fool of herself, but to her surprise it was quiet. All eyes were on her. The girls realized they had never heard Anna talk so much. She felt better, for they were not menacing stares, but stares of respect. And she smiled back at Miss Chadwick, as the next girl stood to give her thanks.

After devotion, everyone was handed a small bouquet of flowers by the matrons. Miss Chadwick went from girl to girl with a hug or a compliment, and told Anna, "Your words were very kind, very soothing. Somehow I feel that this may be your true calling in life. Oration—speaking to people. Oh, it doesn't have to be to the masses, but somehow I know that throughout your life people will look up to you. They will listen. Maybe your message will be from Jesus. Maybe you will speak to the people for Him." Then she hugged her.

Anna settled comfortably into the hug. The two had developed such a special friendship—she almost hated the fact that she was growing up. She knew one day she'd have to leave, and she shuddered at the thought of being alone again. But I won't think about that now she reasoned, as everyone excitedly hurried to the dinning room for their Thanksgiving dinner.

The table was set with the good dishes and in front of each girl's plate was a bag of goodies for after dinner. The turkeys were craved and everyone's plate was filled with meat, dressing, mashed potatoes, corn, sweet potatoes and hot biscuits. They drank cool milk and had peach and cherry cobbler for dessert. Everyone stuffed themselves, much like the turkeys had once been, and needless to say the bags of goodies were untouched for quite a while.

Winter had engaged full time now, but somehow it didn't matter much to the girls. Their new home was warm and cozy and there was no more chopping and carrying kindling for the old stoves.

One day after school, Anna was told she had some mail, so she picked up her letter and retreated to the library to read it before dinner. It was from Essie, so she quickly started to read:

Dear Anna,

You probably thought I was long lost by now, but I want you to know things are okay. I've been traveling about with the Captain and his family, and Anna, you'd be surprised how different some cities are.

Anyway, Captain Jenkins was transferred to Fort Warren, here in Cheyenne, Wyoming, and that's where I live now. It's kinda pretty here, and I was living on post until I met this real nice man. His name is Philip Baker, and even though he's eighteen years older than me, he's real nice. Who knows? Maybe I'm just looking for the father I never had. Anyway Anna, I'm married. Yep, my name is Essie Baker, and he has a nice home, a good car, and enough money to at least make me stay a little while.

I've been in the hospital lately, because I had a miscarriage. That's when you're having a baby and it dies. It hurt a lot, and really bothered me, but I guess the Lord knows that I'm really not the motherly kind. In life I want money, comfort, leisure, and I'm afraid that a bunch of kids would not afford me these things. Anyway the doctors have told me that I'll never be able to have any more children. And here's the irony of it all. I heard that little Carrie, the one I burned with the hot poker, is unable to bare children too. Boy, life sure turns around to face you doesn't it? But Anna, aside from that, things are pretty good for me, although I'll admit I do miss you and the home a lot. I still work for Captain Jenkins and his family, part time, and I've told them all about you and our family. Someday I hope you can meet them.

  I wrote to Aunt Nancy about being married, and she wrote back saying she was happy for me. She says it just might be what I need to calm me down. But I doubt it.

  Anna I'm eighteen now and you're almost fifteen, and I feel like I'm 60. We've been through so much together, and I think it's time we started looking ahead. I'm not sure what your goals are, but I know mine. I will not struggle anymore. I won't be stressed and tired from overwork and not enough food. If there's one thing the orphanage taught me, it's that life can be pleasant. And I want to remember it always, even though my past always seems to creep back to me whenever I feel too happy.

  Did you get your letter from Aunt Nancy? She said she wrote them at the same time. It's kinda sad how her words seem to slant down, off the page, but her hands hurt real bad. Maybe when Philip gets a leave, we will drive down to see her.

  Well, Anna, I'm gonna go for now. Take care, and, yes, say a prayer for me. Tell me. Have you gained any weight yet?

Love,
Essie

Anna sat back and thought about the things she'd just read. "Essie married, children, a husband, Wyoming." She realized now that her sister was in a far different sector of life than she was, for she'd never really thought about those things. She wondered what Essie's baby would have looked like. She wondered what Philip looked like. Yes, Essie had a life of her own now, and again she felt deserted, sad. Not sad for Essie but for herself, and it was then it came to her.

"When I grow up," she thought, "I'm gonna have a hundred children, lots of children, and I'll never be lonely again." With that she brushed away a tear that she hated for falling, and folded the letter carefully, placing it in the pocket closet to her heart. She then went to wash up, knowing dinner was bound to be almost ready.

At dinner she sat quietly as the others chatted eagerly about Christmas, and how much fun it would be here in the new home. One or two off hand remarks were said, but soon they just ignored Anna. They thought she was a bit strange, but accepting that, quiet for her was usually the norm. But she was unaware of the remarks, and she ate her dinner slowly, thinking, "Maybe if they looked real hard, they'd see there's something on my mind. Maybe if they took the time to know me, they'd know that inside it hurts. Then again, maybe if I opened up just a little more to them, they wouldn't feel the need to wonder so much about me. I mean, just how complex can one skinny yellow girl be?" She vowed to figure that out later and continued to eat the rest of her dinner.

That night in bed, she lay with the curtains open slightly, looking at the snow that had found its way about the landscape. The boughs of the big tree outside her window seemed to sigh from their load, but proudly held on to their guest, their out-stretched arms reaching far into the heavens, showing off. The words of the letter went through and through her mind—she was embarrassed by her selfish thoughts of desertion. For didn't Essie have a right to be happy? Didn't she have a right to finally cut the tie? But just exactly what did this mean to her. Was she truly alone now? Anna knew that she was coming of an age that she had to make some decision about her life.

The words of Miss Chadwick floated through her mind: "You must apply yourself," and "With God all things are possible," and she reasoned within herself that all would work out. Besides, in every bad time hadn't someone (all-be-it God, in some shape or manner) always been there? And with this reasoned she again watched the laden tree, but this time she thought Christmas thoughts, and soon she had drifted off to sleep.

At last it was Christmas Eve and the girls stood or mingled about the huge Christmas tree that stood decorated to the hilt in the corner by the fireplace in the library. Bright bulbs sparked like colored stars as they tried to guess just some of the many gifts and toys that lay at its feet. Yes, this was the best of all holidays at the home, and the packages were so far more plentiful than any of the past years.

That evening they drank apple cider and ate popcorn as they wrapped the remainder of their presents and sang carols— the anticipation building as bedtime neared.

In their rooms they chattered endlessly about the next day, and even Anna joined in some, trying desperately not to think so much about Essie and the others. Her only hope was that theirs was as good as hers.

The next morning everyone seemed to wake up early instinctively, reaching for the ledge above their beds, where they knew Miss Chadwick and the matrons had put a special gift as they slept.

The sounds of carols filled their ears from Spellman campus, across the street, and they hurried to dress so they could join the other people.

Racing to the campus entrance, they stood around the beautifully decorated evergreen, and sang the songs of Christmas time, careful to listen for the breakfast bell.

After breakfast, everyone went to the Chapel for a short talk by one of the matrons on what this holiest of days was really for; they listened patiently, but honestly they could barely contain themselves.

Miss Chadwick was never present at the Christmas morning service, and even though all the girls knew why, the excitement was overwhelming.

Soon Chapel was over and there were more bells ringing. Only different bells. Jingle bells and Miss Chadwick burst in wearing her Santa Claus suit. The girls all crowded around her and were led to the library, where there were stacked even more gifts than the night before. So many gifts. They were piled everywhere—even on the fireplace mantel which housed a roaring fire.

After things settled down a bit, each girl's name was called and she went to the tree to get her gifts. There were combs, underwear, stockings, dolls, toys, brushes, new tooth brushes; just so many things that all that could be heard was paper ripping in abandon. There was not a hint of calm, and Miss Chadwick and the matrons smiled as they let the girls have their day. And thanking all for the gifts, Anna opened her packages, giggling, especially relishing the huge book of poetry and short stories from Miss Chadwick.

Opening a small box from Aunt Nancy, she fingered the warm mittens, her mind drifting as it always did on this special day. She hoped Aunt Nancy liked the oven mitt she'd sent her, and Essie, the bright red combs. She hoped Miss Chadwick liked the hankies. Across the room Anna was met with a smile as the woman opened her gift. A smile that meant, this is nice, all's okay, and Anna settled, knowing that everything really was okay.

"Don't dwell, Anna," she thought, as she put the silk stockings from Essie back in their box. "Be content, don't dwell on things that you cannot change, for others are moving on. Don't feel so guilty for feeling happy," she resolved, as she tore into her other presents.

Life was good, calm, and at the home the winter months passed almost uneventfully. Anna excelled in all her classes, and she was now at the age where her skills were often used to assist and teach the younger children.

The new home was kept with pride, and Anna knew that surely no place, no home, could be much better than this.

Everyone was planning a trip. This was a sort of breakfast trip to Historic Stone Mountain, and the matrons were busy packing and preparing all the food they would take with them.

It wasn't a very big mountain and once there, the girls scrambled out of the cars for their climb—unmindful of the drooping clouds they'd passed on their way up. Halfway up, it started to sprinkle but still they climbed as if reaching the top was their destiny.

Once on top, the rain was pouring, and Anna stood high—looking at the clouds, bushes and small trees, like an unspoken hero. But the other girls scurried to get back down. Then finally she started to descend, not caring or maybe not aware that she was soaked to the bone, so rapt was she with God's nature. Once down she was hurried to a car with the other girls, given a cold egg sandwich with bacon, and rushed back to the home so the girls could get out of their wet clothes.

There could be no chances taken with anyone getting sick, as just the month prior, three girls had come down with T.B. and had to be sent to a sanitarium.

All the soggy girls changed clothes and were instructed they could go about their day, but Anna decided just to stay in her room as the long mountain trek had tired her somewhat.

Piling a few good books about her, she pulled a blanket over herself and read as the dripping rain beat muffled messages against the window, and soon she fell asleep.

"You gonna eat lunch?" Catherine asked, as Anna jumped, suddenly conscious and unaware that she had slept so long. "I'll be right there," she answered, readying herself, even though she didn't feel very hungry.

At lunch she picked at her food, then finished her science project before going to the music room to await dinner.

The rain had mostly stopped. Only a slight drizzle remained and Anna watched the other girls as they milled outside the window. Pulling her sweater around her, she wondered how they could be outside running about so. It seemed so cold to her.

After dinner she again retired to her room, where she put on her night clothes and read for awhile. But for some reason, sleep was all too inviting. When she awoke again, it was morning.

Anna declined breakfast. She even declined Chapel services. She was just so cold. She needed to warm up, maybe more blankets, or more socks. Again she dozed, awakened only by the muffled voice of Miss Chadwick, instructing Tugar, "Go get Dr. Holmes, quick. I've lost two girls to T.B. and I don't intend to lose Anna. Let's move her to a private room."

After her examination, Anna lay in the small quiet room—for what seemed like a long time—and listened to Dr. Homes and Miss Chadwick discuss her outside the door.

"This is it!" she thought. "I'm dying and they're afraid to tell me. Oh well, at least I don't have any real sharp pains or anything. I just can't seem to stay awake." And she strained to hear her end results from the hallway.

Miss Chadwick came in, sat down and looked at her directly. "I want you to rest. We'll be bringing some soup in for you to eat," but Anna cut her off.

"Am I dying?" she asked looking the woman squarely in the eye.

"Dying, Oh no!"said Miss Chadwick. Let's just say a lot of years of neglect and abuse has finally caught up to you. Now I'll be in to talk to you in detail later, and get that dying nonsense out of your head." So Anna turned over and went back to sleep.

That night after Anna had some tomato soup and hot tea, Miss Chadwick came in with a clinking bag of bottles, and proceeded to explain to Anna her condition.

"When you first came to us, Anna, many years ago, you were sickly, and you know we've gone to great lengths to try to build you up. You were a very tiny child, and I'm afraid you haven't grown too awfully much, even with all our efforts. Do you remember how, when the other girls ran or played real hard, you generally lagged? Even with hide-an-seek, you found a comfortable place to hide, and just stayed there, rather than tear around like the other girls.

"Your Aunt Nancy told me that when you were quite young, you were blown up by dynamite caps, and this may have something to do with your condition. Or maybe too many cold nights, or poor eating habits. At any rate, Dr. Holmes has informed me that your body, your system, is totally run down and you can no longer adhere to the schedule that you've had. Physically you are just tired out. You have no more strength or energy, and all the doctor can suggest is that we try a little harder to build you up.

"From this day on you are forbidden from any physical work or activity. You must not exert yourself in any shape, form or fashion. If you feel tired, you are to rest. The doctor says you are not to be pushed to study too hard. When the girls go on excursions, you cannot participate; no hiking, no swimming— nothing.

"Anna, this is for your own good, plus it's doctor's orders. You just have no strength left and we're trying all we know to try to build you back up some. Now, every day you must do exactly as I say, and take this Scott's Emulsion faithfully. Every single day.

"I know you always wanted more energy, and hated the fact that you weren't quite as rough or energetic as the other girls. I also know that you were trying to prove a point when you stayed on the mountain so long. So now we have to try and undo a slight bit of foolishness, and with God, the Scott's, and your cooperation, we'll pull you through this problem, too."

From then on Anna's activities were very few. She was put on office duty, while the others took swimming lessons, or she listened to the Victrola, or just sat and read, which was, in fact, her favorite thing to do.

Sometimes when there were no appointments, or all office work was caught up, Anna would do sewing room duty. She thought this was fun and she loved working with Miss Fenicle.

Sometimes Anna was allowed to take over the sewing classes, instructing the girls how to sew, and often helping to sew the younger girls clothing. She'd also assist the older girls, who made their own dresses and nice things for their rooms. The girls particularly liked to sew bedspreads made out of unbleached muslin, embroidered with flowers, and colored with crayolas. They were then pressed with a hot iron to make sure the colors had set in.

Anna thought this was great to see pretty results from a mere piece of muslin, and she delighted in the outcome. Miss Fenicle had taught her well.

As bad as things had seemed to be, they worked out well. Even though Anna could no longer rip and run, and climb or swim, she was still very productive and doing a lot of the things that she still loved.

The change in her schedule had afforded Anna much time to read and study. Her papers were impeccable, and Anna could see that it was causing a bit of a rift with the other girls. They whispered over the fact that Anna's life was now privileged, but never noticed the fact that she also missed an awful lot of fun, and took an awful lot of Scott's Emulsion.

Anna was sixteen now and her activities, or lack thereof, were slowly taking their toll. After all there was only so much sewing that you can do. But just in time, something else had sparked her interest. Word was that there was a contest starting in the school. A Biblical speaking contest, open to all. Many girls entered, but Anna and Frances Brock from Pasadena, California, were the finalist. Frances was in college and an eloquent speaker, but Anna was undaunted. Besides, this time, this one time, all the girls were pulling for her.

Miss Chadwick rehearsed with Anna almost every day, stressing that there had to be expression and perfect diction. Every punctuation had to be noted and emphasized.

"Always remember," she told her, "to drop your voice at a period, pause at a comma, slightly raise at a question, and show self assertiveness that comes only with knowing that you are the best." And Anna believed her. She knew that if she did anything well at all, it was speaking.

The big day finally arrived, and the girls from the school and some from colleges gathered noisily in the assembly hall. Anna and Frances stood back stage, looking first at each other, and then away—not sure whether to associate or not—but aware that there was an air of respect between them.

Miss Chadwick walked on the stage and the hall fell suddenly silent, like a needle quickly lifted from the phonograph. All listened as she read the rules of the contest. She congratulated both girls on being finalists and announced that the rules were the same for both. They were to recite St. John, the 14th chapter, the 23 Psalm, and the 1st of Proverbs, from verse 10 to the end of the chapter. Then she announced that Frances would speak first.

You could hear a pin drop as the girl walked on stage, her heel's clickin' rhythmically against the shinny linoleum floor. She started, her voice strong, perfect, assured. Anna listened back-stage, her heart pounding as the words rang louder in her ears than they actually were. Then she heard it. The mistake.

Anna's eyes flit to the judges who sat in a row, following along in their Bibles. They marked short dashes on slim pieces of paper and she knew they'd caught it too. But Frances kept right on speaking, either covering the fact, or unaware of the fact that she had neglected to pause at a comma. She finished her verses clearly, and bowed to the audience as she exited the stage, glancing at Anna briefly. A glance that made Anna know that she knew of the error.

Again the crowd was silent as Anna walked on stage, mindful not to let her heels tap on the floor. The podium seemed miles away but she walked straight, her head high, like the time they'd walked from the town with new shoes. Her mind raced ahead somewhat, but she was careful not to let it settle on that nightmare comma.

She started speaking with the air of eloquence that only comes with good breeding or much learning. She recited the 23rd Psalm, with not a flaw. Proverbs—perfectly. She then commenced to St. John. The audience was awed. In St. John, she spoke of Jesus comforting his disciples on his impending death, beginning with, "Let not your heart be troubled, ye believe in God, believe also in me." He promised that he was going to prepare a place for his followers, and that he would come again and receive them unto Himself. Anna looked around, her voice lifting, and she knew she held them in her power. By the time she reached the last verse they were spellbound.

She knew it. Then she came to the end as Jesus, speaking to his disciples, said, "Arise, let us go hence". Her tones rose and then fell to the occasion. It was over. The audience sat hushed, silent, rapt. Moments passed, small eons, then they all burst into boisterous applause. How they clapped and cheered, as Anna moved back from the podium, her head dizzy with the triumph of winning. Yes, this was truly a time of sheer triumph.

The prize was $10.00. On commencement day in the beautiful new chapel, Anna waited breathlessly for her name to be called, then almost floated to the altar, to receive the prize. She sent it to Aunt Nancy for all her love and understanding, and teaching in the past.

It was mail call and Anna rushed to pass it out so she could open her own two letters. One sender was unknown to her, but the other was Aunt Nancy, so she decided to save it for last. They always tugged at her heart so.

Tearing open the manila envelope, she found it was from a person who had heard her verses and wished for her to enter a nationwide contest. Anna folded up the letter, her head spinning. Maybe she would save this one until last, she thought as she opened Aunt Nancy's letter on the way to the library. Aunt Nancy told of how things were and were not, and who'd gotten saved and who died. She told of canning pickle-lilly and grape jam and how Essie had just written to say she had a car. She said Essie loved Cheyenne, Wyoming, but still hankered for Georgia at times. It seemed Uncle Mayo was having a time of things. He was sick but she was trying to nurse him out of it. And, as always, she said, she had not heard from Doc or Roosevelt but she knew they were well, safe and in God's hands. She always ended with her love, her pride in Anna, and her never-ending faith in God.

Anna put the letter back in the envelope. Even after all this time, they still always tended to make her cry. Not because she was really unhappy or miserable here, but because even through all that had been done for her, even though she'd grown up here, she still longed for the feel of real family. Flesh and blood family. She sat back and thought of Uncle Mayo. She thought of being five years old and sitting in the train station, hour after hour, all day waiting for the tall brown man who never came. It's funny how that stayed in her memory, even though she'd found out later that it was all a mistake. Uncle Mayo had misunderstood and gone to the station the following day, where he, too, had waited all day only to go back alone. It seems they were always just missing each other in one way or another. Anna remembered the few letters he'd written as she was growing up. "I'm workin' real hard, little one," he would say." And when you come out of the orphanage, I'll have a fine home all ready and waitin' for you."

But Anna knew that no matter how well intended, these things would probably never be. And now he was sick. She wasn't sure how sick, because Aunt Nancy never really told the real extent of things. So Anna knew that when she wrote back to tell about the contest, and the latest news, she'd have to ask for exact details about Uncle Mayo, and about Aunt Nancy. She couldn't help feeling that there was more to the letter than was told.

Heading for Miss Chadwick's office she knocked lightly on the door, then handed her the small manila envelope. Miss Chadwick read the letter, said nothing, then read it again. She smiled.

"This is wonderful Anna," she said. "Someone besides me has finally recognized your talent. The only thing that worries me is your health. You know you aren't well and this is such a big task. I'll admit it's a great opportunity, but it will take lots of reading and research, and with the four pounds that you've recently lost, I just don't know if you're up to it."

Anna thought for just a moment about the task that lay ahead of her. And she knew that if her true means of self worth lay in her orations, then this was meant to be. "I want to compete, Miss Chadwick. I want to more than anything right now," she reasoned, waiting for a more favorable response.

"Then so be it," said Miss Chadwick, "Now sit down and prepare an answer to their query so we can mail it right away. After all, you've got quite a project cut out for you."

Anna smiled and rushed out, with a hasty "*Thank you*," eager to get the ball rolling.

Days passed. Anna poured through what appeared to be tons of material and information, learning much along the way, but still undecided as to what to title her essay. Her discoveries were fascinating, and she knew she would remember them always. One particularly warm night as Anna lay in bed, her mind drifted through all she'd read. She focused on an article that she'd read in the black newspaper some time ago. It read, "Every tenth person in America is a Negro. "That's it!" she said, almost out loud. "My essay will be titled <u>America's 10th Man-The Black Man</u>. With this finally established, she knew falling asleep would be easier this night.

Anna was up early. With the title firmly planted in mind, it was far easier to know which route to take in writing. Black History, Explorers, Singers, Poets, Writers, Slaves, so much, so very much, needed to be heard.

A few weeks passed and soon the work was completed and on Miss Chadwick's desk for approval. Anna sat stiffly across from her, fidgeting with her shoes and oozing impatience, until she was ushered out and told to attend to her chores in the office and return in a couple of hours. She did as she was told, walking slowly down the hall, as Miss Chadwick called after her not to forget her medicine.

"I won't," called back Anna, knowing full well she hadn't taken the potion for a couple of weeks.

Later Miss Chadwick joined her, letter in hand, beaming. She could only smile, and nod her approval to the small young girl who had grown so wise, before her eyes.

"This is it," she whispered. "It goes directly to the council. It's time the truth is told."

Soon, Anna found herself again in front of her peers. Her words were soft, yet direct, and biting as she spoke so eloquently about that which she'd come to admire so much. Her race. Her people.

This done, all that was left to do was wait for their reply and hope they understood. Some time later, two letters came again; one from the council, the other from back home. Anna opened the council letter first, excited with the anticipation of winning, but nervous in spite of herself. The other letter she put in her pocket for later.

Dear Anna, We have carefully reviewed your well given and researched speech, and while we think it was exceptional in every way, we have chosen as our winner another participant. Your very worthwhile effort was given an honorable mention. Please keep up the good work, and we hope your public speaking leads you far.
Sincerely

Anna folded up the delicate perfumed paper and walked to the back porch, hoping it was empty. She hated to lose. Hated it, and she needed to escape, to cope with her anger. "They couldn't possibly have understood my message," she reasoned. "They're little people with little minds that can't see beyond here and now. They don't want to believe about America's tenth man. That's it. They don't want to believe that we're a voice to be reckoned with, a voice to be heard. They're just not quite ready for me yet." Then she settled back in the swing, sinking into what was only her world.

She must have dozed, for the sun was sinking, allowing only a minimum of light. Feeling a little chilly she pushed her hands in her pockets, and only then did she remember the letter from home. The letter from Aunt Nancy. She opened the folded paper, and although it was far less attractive than the other letter, it was surely more endearing. She started to read. It was short and she read quickly, her eyes stinging as she re-folded the letter and headed for Miss Chadwick's office—the words "come home," ringing in her head.

Miss Chadwick was not in her office. Anna found her in the music room, by the window, her eyes closed just slightly, listening to the music. Anna walked over slowly, quietly, careful not to break the melodic trance her mentor seemed so rapt in. And she didn't move until the last strains of the composition had drifted out the window. Then she carefully whispered, "Miss Chadwick," and put the letter in her hand.

Miss Chadwick read the letter, then folded it precisely and put it back in the envelope saying, "Prepare to go, Anna, and be sure to contact Essie, as I'm sure she'll want to meet you there. There are some things that I'd intended to tell you in the coming week but they can't wait now. A couple of weeks ago I had cause to contact Essie about a certain matter, and a few things have been settled. Also, even though I was asked not to say so, I feel you can handle this news. You've grown up now, Anna. I know within that tiny body is an inner strength that few could contain. Times change, Anna, and we change with them, although not always for the best.

"It's Aunt Nancy. I know she doesn't mention it in her letters to you, but I've learned she's not well. You know how vague she sometimes is, unwilling to talk much about herself, but I've read between the lines. So when you're home, just watch her closely, carefully. She's been so busy with others all these years that she's more than neglected her own self. Now run along and prepare your things for your trip. With things as dire as they are, you are to leave no later than tomorrow—early evening."

Anna turned to walk away, not sure whether to scream or cry about the news she'd just heard. Uncle Mayo dying. It seemed so unbelievably sad. Shy, forgetful, quiet Uncle Mayo, who was always there, who always managed to slip a dime in the letters. And Aunt Nancy. Dear God, there could be no thought of losing Aunt Nancy. She was part of the reason Anna had strived to excel. Aunt Nancy, with her love and strength, was the reason she always walked that extra mile. This fine education was for her, so Anna could support her and buy her the pretty things that had always seemed to elude her. She had to stay strong. Anna had too much to show her.

Miss Chadwick broke her thought. "Did you hear me, Anna? Are you listening? I said that when you're at home, talk some with Essie, listen a little. I feel that marriage and life have matured her, and for once, Essie and I do agree on something. Now go prepare for your trip." Anna nodded, staring again into the eyes that seemed so familiar to her.

In her room she placed the brown worn suitcase on the bed and proceeded to fill it with the starched clean uniforms from the drawer. She filled it with leggings, her good shoes, her bible, and a brown bag of peppermints. She folded her best dress, for she knew she'd have to wear it. Although the other girls stared at her, she said nothing. And they went along with that, having learned years ago that this was just Anna. Then pushing the suitcase against the wall, she put on her nightclothes and sat on the end of the bed, facing the window. Her heart felt so sad, and although she would be glad to see home again, she knew that somehow this trip was different. Somehow things would just never be the same. Leaning back and crying quietly, she thought, "Why's life always so sad?" And she wiped the tears and tried to forget the look in those familiar eyes.

Anna fidgeted as she stood by the front door, suitcase in tow, waiting for the car to pull around. She fingered her stiff collar that had too much starch, and looked down at the bags that had gathered in the knees of her leggings. "All grown up, huh?" she thought to herself. "Then why don't my knees and chest know that?" She almost felt silly, but soon noticed there were a few girls around her, so she straightened up.

"So scary," some said, or "Be strong, hurry back," and Anna thought to herself, "Good Lord, he's not dead yet." But she still graciously accepted all of their condolences as Miss Chadwick handed her a box lunch, and ushered her to the car, giving instructions. Anna got in and rolled down the window to look at the woman whose sadness matched hers. Miss Chadwick patted her hands, stepped back, and the large black car started down the road to the station.

On the train Anna indeed felt grown up, putting her luggage overhead, and choosing a seat of her own choice. She propped her head against the back rest and stared out the window. The world had changed some, for she hadn't been home in such a long time. If it wasn't for the seriousness of this trip, things could have almost been nice.

When she awoke, it was full dark. She wasn't sure how long she'd slept, but she knew she was hungry. She was glad no one had sat down beside her because she didn't feel much like being polite. She only wanted silence and the train sounds that clicked so rhythmically into the night. Then sitting the boxed lunch on her lap, she pulled the string, pulling back the flaps, eager to see what awaited. There were several sandwiches, peanut butter and syrup, and a tuna sandwich thick with salad dressing and pickles. There was a thick slab of ham on long bread with mustard, and slices of potatoes fried crisp. Apples, oranges and a piece of cake sat to one side, the other holding a tin thermos filled with milk.

And Anna set to task. Eating all she could but careful to leave enough for the next day.

As she got off the train, luggage in hand, she looked around for a face she might recognize. Then she saw her, late as usual, running towards her—grinning. It was Essie. And she was beautiful—tan and beautiful. Her face looked like those girls in the books, unreal and perfect, and she giggled as she spun Anna around. Then ever so coyly batting long black eyelashes, she said, "Little sister, the first thing we have to do is get rid of that uniform. Anna, you haven't changed a bit." But Essie had. Her wavy hair was pinned up at the neck, her pouty mouth red with coloring. She had a chest, and legs that were long and slim in heeled shoes. Anna felt like Raggedy Ann.

As they neared the house, so many memories engulfed her that Anna felt an odd lump in her throat. All of a sudden she was a child again. She wanted to see her Aunt Nancy, she wanted to cry. When the car pulled up front, she jumped out, bursting in the door, soaking up the smell, the look, the feel of the place that she had left so long ago. And there she stood. The same hair, the same face, the same eyes. The same smell of sweet honeysuckle that tingled your nostrils as you buried your head in her strong arms. And Anna cried, if for no other reason than she loved this woman so. She missed her so. She understood her so. And Essie gave them this moment as she quietly tiptoed pass them, taking the luggage to the small room off the kitchen.

Standing in the darkened room at the foot of the bed, Anna stared at the face of the Uncle she adored. The covers were pulled up to his chin and his face looked small and hollow. His eyes were closed just barely, not blinking or fluttering, but not opening either. He hardly moved at all except to say he was cold and to ask for a cup of water. Anna obliged, carefully tilting his head to the tin cup. Then he clasped his hands over hers on the cup and opened his eyes. Not for long, but long enough to see that it was Anna.

Uncle Mayo didn't drink much water, so Anna layed his grey curly head back on the huge pillow. It seemed to engulf him like a still cloud. Then reaching in the cedar chest she put another wool blanket on him. He was so cold. Even though the early evening was quiet warm, he was cool, like the feel of the tin cup when filled with water. Anna pulled up a seat and sat down, resting her head on the edge of the bed. She knew what this meant.

Her mind went way back to Uncle Mayo's words after he'd missed her at the train station. "I'll work real hard Anna, and before you're ready to come out of this orphanage, I'll have a good home all ready for you. I'll try to find a way to provide for you so you won't be alone." But it never came to be. He'd worked so hard just trying to make ends meet, that he could barely provide for himself. But Anna loved him, she loved the short letters that were few and far between. And the extra dimes he tucked between the pages.

"Wake up, Anna. Get up honey," came the sound of Aunt Nancy's voice. Anna jumped, thinking she was dreaming. But she wasn't. She was here at home, and Aunt Nancy was standing there—smiling. Anna had fallen asleep, and stood teetering, still half-asleep and tired from her trip. It was early morning, say two or three a.m., and Aunt Nancy was urging her to go to bed.

Anna stood up and leaned down to Uncle Mayo to make sure his chest was still moving. Slowly it still rose, but he was just so still, so quiet. "Go to bed now," Aunt Nancy told her, as she hugged her. "I'll sit the rest of the night with Mayo. Since you were here, it allowed me to get some sleep. Now come with me."

Anna leaned into her Auntie and was half walked, half carried to the small room, and Nancy helped her with her shoes, and then she quickly changed into a long muslin gown and got beneath the covers. She felt sleep taking over as soon as she touched the pillow and she allowed it its reign, as Aunt Nancy gently kissed her pale cheek. Then she left her alone with her thoughts and the smell of sweet honeysuckle.

The next morning Anna slept late, and awoke with a jolt, not quite remembering where she was. A cool breeze blew through the window, and Anna looked around at the small room off the kitchen. It really hadn't seemed to change at all. Jumping up, she closed the window against the gale that she felt was cool. She looked out. Hay was stacked, wood was piled, and the outhouse was still out back. It looked so sadly wonderful to her.

Turning to the peeling night stand, Anna washed up in the small basin of warm water placed there conveniently by her Aunt Nancy. Greeting, then rushing past her Aunt in the kitchen, Anna went straight to Uncle Mayo's room.

Again she put her ear close to his mouth and chest to hear his breathing. It seemed so much slower and fainter. Then he spoke, clearly, just above a whisper, but loud enough to fill the quiet room.

"Hello child," he murmured. "I saw you here the other day. I knew you'd be here. I'm still gonna get the house." But Anna stopped him.

"I know you will Uncle Mayo. But right now you have to rest. Just rest. I'm gonna go get a bite to eat, then I'll be right back to sit and read to you." Uncle Mayo nodded, and Anna left the room with a small chill running through her like the breeze from the room off the kitchen.

In the kitchen Aunt Nancy stood with her back against the cupboard, so immersed in thought that Anna almost startled her. "I'm sorry I slept so long," Anna said, but her Aunt quickly assured her it was okay. Then pointing to a seat at the too big kitchen table, she instructed Anna to sit down to a meal of yellow grits, bacon, eggs, toast, grape jam, and buttermilk. "Gotta put some meat on that tiny body," Aunt Nancy told her. Anna set to her meal, breaking up her bacon in the grits and piling the scrambled eggs on top. Aunt Nancy poured a glass of buttermilk and sat down with her news of this and that, but Anna just ate and stared at this wonderful woman before her. "When did she get so small?" thought Anna, remembering the robust woman with the big smile, who could almost smother you with a hug. But the eyes were still the same.

Anna sat and read to Uncle Mayo most of the afternoon, never really sure if he was actually hearing her.

But that didn't matter. The fact that she was even in the same room with him was all that was important to her.

When she was sure he was asleep, she quietly left the room, dimming the kerosene lamp and closing the door behind her. Hearing the porch chair creak, she grabbed a sweater, peeked at the pots on the stove, then joined Aunt Nancy on the porch. How this brought back memories—memories of laughter and fear, pain, great joy, memories of love. There was a much needed silence for a while as the two sat together on the large porch bench that Uncle Mayo had converted to a rocker.

Laying her head on her Aunt's shoulder, Anna finally spoke, almost fishing for words, unsure of how to begin.

"Aunt Nancy," she started. "I noticed in the kitchen, you were cooking greens with whole potatoes and ham hocks. I know you're real busy what with Uncle Mayo and all, but you are managing to save some food for yourself, aren't you? You are eating okay, aren't you?"

Aunt Nancy looked down at her and smiled. "I suppose you're referring to why I've lost some weight? Well, I'm eating just fine. I just needed to get a bit off of me, that's all. Now you're not about to go worrying about that, are you?"

"No, ma'am," assured Anna as she tucked her legs beneath her on the rocker. She felt like a child, and it was cozy to sit here nestled against her Aunt Nancy, even though there was far less of her with which to nestle.

"You're always thinking, aren't you?" her Aunt asked her. "Always so wise. And where are your freckles, girl? When did your hair turn brown?"

"I'm not sure," Anna responded. "I guess I haven't paid that must attention," and Aunt Nancy chuckled, careful not to break the spell of a moment they may never have again. After a while, Anna spoke.

"Where's Essie?" she asked. "Didn't she sleep here last night?"

"Oh no child!" was the answer. "Since Essie's been back, she stays mostly up to Dolly's place. But she should be here directly."

"And what about Papa?" Anna asked, half wanting, half not wanting to know.

"Jim, well I hear that he's still around," Nancy told her. Jim will always be just Jim. I've seen him just a few times, and he acted like he didn't see me, though I know full well that he did. Jim always did know better than to start with me," she half chuckled.

"Still it's sad, Anna," she continued. "He's my brother and, believe it or not, I can still remember when we were young, a much different Jim. Ah, you should have seen him then, tall, and handsome. Every girl near abouts liked him, but Lula won his heart. It's a shame he allowed them others to come between them. From what I hear, he just sits and drinks mostly. Miss Carrie's been long gone. It's funny how she just had to have him. Just had to run Lula off. Then when she did, he actually hated her for it. Her life, those childrens' lives, was miserable. I'm not sure where they are now. You know, Jim never got over losing everything. Especially you. Still, I'll bet there's some idiot woman, still in his face trying to make him happy. Jim will always be Jim," she trailed off as she got up from the bench and walked towards the door.

"I know he'll never forgive me," she said with a sigh, as she looked back at Anna, who had kept her seat. "Yet I know when they tell me that he's down, I'll be there to help him. He's my brother. But I just couldn't leave you children to live in such a mess. Essie will be here directly. Just sit here and wait for her. I'm going on in to Uncle Mayo."

Anna sat for a minute or two, but for some reason, she felt even cooler now. In her mind she saw the face of the man she had feared so. She thought about the running and the threats. She also thought about Christmas long ago and the Christmas stocking.

She followed her Aunt into the house, not wanting to be alone on the porch. She was filled with different emotions, some scary but mostly sad. She knew she despised him for what he'd done to her mother, to her, to her family, but she still couldn't understand the love and sadness that overwhelmed her about her father.

Anna went into the living room just to sit around for a while and feel the familiar. She ignored the faded doilies, thinking how nice Aunt Nancy tried to make things even though she had little of nothing to work with. Things may have been old or faded, but they were clean and orderly and the sharp smell of homegrown collards filled the house.

After going into the small room to get paper and pencil, Anna returned to the living room and sat on the faded, worn couch.

Dear Miss Chadwick, I arrived safely and I must say I miss you and the girls and the home a lot. I love being here with my family, but you are my family too. Uncle Mayo's really not doing well, so this will be a short note, because I want to go back in his room and sit with Aunt Nancy. Essie's fine. She's really pretty and, well she's still Essie. I'll write more later; oh, and Miss Chadwick, I love you.
Anna

She put the note in an envelope she'd addressed, checked the food on the stove, then went back in the room with her Aunt Nancy and Uncle Mayo.

They sat for quite a while as Aunt Nancy read scriptures and quotes from the Bible. Padding the stiff wooden chair with a blanket, Anna tried to absorb every word and its meaning from the lips of her aunt. Her voice almost sang like a lark. Soon early evening was upon them, spewing just enough gold and red through the darkened room to be breathtaking.

Aunt Nancy leaned over. "Go set the table, child," she told Anna. "Mayo's asleep now, but I'll just sit a bit longer." Anna nodded and got up from her chair, looking down at her Uncle's face and chest before she left the room.

Anna was nearly through setting the table, when she heard a car pull up. "Essie!" she thought, as she raced out the door and across the dirt path to the car. The girls giggled, Essie tossing her wavy hair back from her face.

"Girl, look at you!" she said, grinning at Anna. "You're actually growing up. And your hair doesn't look like stewed tomatoes anymore," she teased, messin' Anna's hair that always stayed tousled. "Why, with a little fixing up, I'll bet the boys would just fall all over you." Somehow Anna doubted that.

"Are you still married, Essie?" Anna asked her. "I have so many things I need to ask you. In driving around, are you afraid you may run into Papa? Why is Aunt Nancy so small now? What do you and Miss Chadwick talk about?"

Essie leaned back against the car and sighed, and it was a moment before she started to speak.

"Yes I am married," she said. "I am still Essie Baker, but he's on the go with the railroad a lot so I make do without him. He's nice. If I ran into Papa, well, I'd probably shoot him. I would, I know I would, and as far as Aunt Nancy's losing weight, I just figured as people got older, they naturally got thinner or smaller."

"Good Lord, I hope not," said Anna out loud, and the sisters laughed as they walked towards the house, having noticed Aunt Nancy in the doorway.

Dinner was a twitter of guests and fond memories. And even some half-truths, mostly told by Essie. Word had pretty much spread about Uncle Mayo, and people stopped by to bring food and condolences to the family. Miss Banks brought chitlins and pone, which Anna hated. Miss Kearney brought a huge mincemeat pie, which Essie hated, but those things didn't matter, in these times. The callers marveled at Nancy's girls, and the girls vaguely remembered some of them. The few young men who had gathered simply marveled at Essie, but Anna understood. Standing back against the wall, she watched as Aunt Nancy served and Essie smiled and she almost forgot. But that was all right. Uncle Mayo was dying, and she only hoped that everyone remembered why they'd come.

Anna slipped into her Uncle's room, and pulled up a chair, mindful of the din in the other rooms. His eyes were closed and he was still, but breathing. Anna wondered if he could hear any of his friends. His friends, Aunt Nancy's friends, her father's friends. She wondered if he'd come. Surely he knew by now. His brother was dying. Wouldn't he want, or need to say *a good-bye*? Uncle Mayo had always been so kind.

Soon the door opened slightly and Essie slipped inside. "Get up," she whispered. "Let's pad that hard chair with this blanket." Then they settled in, both girls fitting snugly in the wooden chair.

Off and on different people filtered in and out of the room, but the girls were mostly quiet, preferring to give everyone their moment. Some prayed with him, some talked to him, some just sat and held his hands, but love was everywhere. Uncle Mayo smiled some, but spoke very little, and when he did it was in a halting voice.

The girls still sat as Aunt Nancy came in, scooting her chair closer to the bed, her hair somewhat mussed from the rigor of the guests.

"Has he spoke much?" she asked the girls, and Essie responded.

"Aunt Nancy, why are people asking him questions he can't possibly answer? Can't they see they're tiring him out?"

Uncle Mayo half smiled. "Hush, girl, you behave yourself," he scolded, and Essie jumped up and hugged him, as she headed out the door.

"I think I'll corner Essie and have her help me clean the kitchen," Anna said as she stood up brushing back her Aunt's hair. "You sit in here and rest a bit with Uncle Mayo. I'm sure with Essie in there, she can entertain those folks enough to keep them occupied for a while," and she followed her sister out of the room.

Anna got started, collecting plates and glasses, cups and platters, carrying them in several trips to the kitchen, and after a while Essie reluctantly joined in. With all the dishes piled about them they got busy.

"Make it fun, sister!" Anna said, and Essie stopped in her tracks, looking at her sibling like she was crazy.

"This is filthy food," she barked. "Other peoples,' some strangers,' dirty plates. This is not fun."

And Anna spoke right up. "It was when we were little," and for just a small second Anna saw in her sister's face her father's eyes. Then both girls turned around, the yellowing linoleum creaking behind them. There stood three young men. They couldn't have been more than eighteen or nineteen, just standing there. Anna thought they looked stupid, and Essie saw a chance to play her role.

"Oh, little sister," she cooed, then proceeded to mangle Anna's hair with a soap filled hand.

Anna was livid. That's all she needed was her hair bashed down like brown mustard plaster, but she said nothing. Essie knew, in the name of showing out, she had overstepped her bounds, but she just went on, to the delight of her audience, flitting around the kitchen like a speckled butterfly.

As they finished the kitchen, Essie continued her charade, and Anna continued her silence in front of the threesome.

"Watch it, Anna, your ears are getting red," Essie teased, snickering and lowering her voice.

"No, you watch it, Essie!" Anna countered loudly as she slammed her upside the head with a handful of suds. Then turned, walking past the mute admirers into her room, she slammed the door behind her.

Rinsing the hardened suds from her hair in the basin, Anna doctored her hair as best she could. It was short so it was easy, but the hair was now bushy where the suds had been. Opening her bag, she put some hair grease on the scalp and ends and brushed it back. Right now she didn't much care what it looked like.

She sat for a while then decided she'd go back in with her Aunt Nancy and Uncle Mayo. As she walked through the living room, she noticed a number of the people had left and she was glad. Essie was still holding court with a couple of guys and Anna walked right passed them.

In the room the lamp was dim, and Aunt Nancy sat holding her brother's hand. Her eyes looked watery. So did his.

"He's been calling for you, Anna," she told her. "I was getting ready to come get you. Now I want you to go get Essie and any of the others that wish to see Mayo." Anna did as she was told, feeling nervous inside, and dreading her return to the room. She pulled Essie aside, gave her instructions and went back to her chair, as they filed in, bending to whisper to Aunt Nancy.

Anna got up from her seat, and ushered an elderly neighbor to a seat, then took a place by the window. Uncle Mayo spoke quietly to a number of them, but soon she heard her name being called.

"He wants Anna," someone said. Miss Banks took Anna's arm, escorting her to the side of the bed. It was so quiet, and he looked so far away as she held his cool hand, leaning against the bed board.

"Anna?" he started, his voice low and barely audible. "Is this Anna?"

"Yes Uncle Mayo," she answered, making sure she showed none of the anguish that she felt inside.

"Seek ye first the kingdom of God and His Righteousness and all these things shall be added unto you," he advised her in his slow hushed tone, and she bent down, the tears falling as she whispered.

"I promise I will." Then she took her place back by the window.

It was a long night. Different people took shifts sleeping, always making sure someone was with Uncle Mayo. Around six in the morning Aunt Nancy gently awakened Anna and Essie, who had curled up on the couch, and told them their Uncle was gone.

The girls got up from the couch, hugged their Aunt Nancy and went into the small room off the kitchen. The house was quiet, still, except for the muffled cries that came and went. And the girls cried deeply into the pillows, mourning the Uncle Mayo they had loved so.

The day of Uncle Mayo's funeral was calm and bright, the cool breezes that had proceeded, out of respect, giving way to a still-warmth. Everyone stood around in stiff dresses and starched collars, mumbling lowly, as if they were afraid they'd wake someone up. A steady stream of food filtered into the kitchen and a lot of smells. The small wooden church that housed Uncle Mayo's body was a short walk from the house for Aunt Nancy and the girls, so along with those that had gathered, they started over.

Anna wore a simple but pretty dress, her shoes shiny and comfortable, her face scrubbed—pale and somber. Essie's dress was simple too, long and willowy, her face daubed with just a hint of rogue, her small heels kicking up the dirt as she walked.

Soft music hummed in the small church as everyone took their seats. Uncle Mayo's wooden casket sat in front of the family, as he slept there, forever still, in front of them.

Anna stared at his face, all brown and kind. He looked so calm, all the gray-look was gone, the labored breathing over. He looked at peace, and somehow as a small choir sang, *"I'm Going Up Yonder,"* Anna felt much better inside.

A number of people stood up and spoke about Uncle Mayo, and Anna held onto their every word. She just didn't realize how much he'd done for so many. Aunt Nancy didn't speak, but sat between Anna and Essie crying softly, her mind drifting to other things. She thought of the plantation and the cool lemonade that she and Mayo used to drink out by the fence with Fanny and Jim. She thought of how the same pain that so enraged Jim only made Mayo more sensible. Mayo, Fanny, almost everyone gone now, except her and Jim. And Jim was as good as gone.

The minister was speaking now. Anna remembered his face, and his voice. He was real old now but his sound was so soothing, so reassuring when he spoke of Uncle Mayo, and of heavens promise, that she just somehow felt better. She looked at Essie, who cried quietly into a lace hankie, and then further down the pew at the many faces whom she knew just had to be family. She quickly glanced around the room half wanting, but not really wanting to see if her dad would show. He didn't.

The cemetery was at the bottom of a slight hill, out back of the old church, and Uncle Mayo's casket led the procession to his final resting place. Small patches of flowers were scattered about and Anna picked several sorts and layed them on top of the casket, whispering, "Good-by Uncle Mayo. I love you." Then she turned and walked away to the large bent oak that stood oddly at the base of the hill.

Leaning against the tree she looked up through the leaves, at the warm sun, as the hymns sung low and sweet filled the air. As the men took the ropes to lower him in, Anna turned away, looking instead at the crest of the hill. She closed her eyes hard, blinking the salty tears onto her face, and she whispered her mother's name.

"Momma," she cried. "Momma, hold me." Then she opened her eyes to the top of the hill, as if she was beckoned.

Against the sun and through her tears, a lone figure stood there, tall, thin, and almost shadowy. It was a man. A gaunt outline of a man, who slowly walked away, as the last strains of the song was sung, and Mayo was lowered to his rest.

Everyone started to walk away and Essie and Aunt Nancy caught up to Anna. As they walked towards the house, each girl holding their Aunt's hand, Anna in a voice barely above a whisper, spoke up.

"I saw someone," she started. "At the top of the hill, watching. I saw him, watching," and Essie cut her off.

"I know," she said softly.

"I know," and Aunt Nancy just kept on walking.

Back at the house, a number of people stood around talking and eating and asking a million questions about the girls. They found that they had a lot of relatives, and they greeted them all respectfully, but they scarcely remembered many of them. Anna retreated to her room.

A few of the ladies from the church had not gone to the funeral, but stayed behind to tend to the food and tidy up things a bit. They had packed some of Uncle Mayo's things away, and changed the sheets that he had died on.

Anna laid back against the pillow and noticed they had freshly changed her bed, too. Her heart was racing. Her insides were sad and scared, and she never heard Essie come in the room.

Essie laid across the bed, fluffing up a pillow and looking at her sister. "I don't want to talk about it," she said, her voice tense and low. "I just don't want to talk about anything right now," and Anna complied. So both girls just lay there thinking themselves to sleep.

The time that Anna had left their home was both sad and sweet. She went a few places with Essie, but mostly she preferred to just hang around the house and help Aunt Nancy.

She'd sent several letters to Miss Chadwick, and on cool nights read her responses to her family. Miss Chadwick's letters were always so detailed and full of news that both Essie and Aunt Nancy loved hearing them. But soon it was time for Anna to return to Spellman, and on that evening, Anna's feelings were almost overwhelming. She was so torn between wanting to go and wanting to stay, but she knew she had to finish her education.

Aunt Nancy had fixed her a good lunch of meat pie, biscuits, syrup and buttermilk, and Essie was to pick her up and take her to the station.

The last hour was so hard. She loved Aunt Nancy so much. They spent the time on the porch, in the big chair that Uncle Mayo had converted. It was quiet as Anna sat nestled by her Aunt, and she wanted it that way. She always felt like a child again at home.

Essie pulled up early, in a hurry, saying she needed to stop by Dolly's on the way to the station. And the lump was there. That wrenching lump in Anna's throat that always managed to travel to her heart when she was with Aunt Nancy.

At the car Anna clung to her shrunken frame as if it were for the last time. All her life, from the plantation on, Aunt Nancy had cared for others. She never married, she never had children. She never complained, and as Anna held her, she prayed that now she would take this time for herself. But in her heart, she knew that soon there would be some sick man, woman or child who Aunt Nancy would take under her wing.

Anna rolled down the window, and touched Aunt Nancy's face. She cried, they both did, as Essie stayed quietly in the driver's seat.

"I love you," Anna whispered. "I'll be back to see you," and the car pulled off, leaving behind the home, the woman, and the eyes that she loved so much.

Essie was staying a few more days before heading back to Cheyenne, and the two sisters drove in silence down the dusty road. She handed Anna a dainty hanky, but said nothing as they passed the church, then the cemetery where she nodded a final good-by to Mayo. They passed the small hill where the stranger had stood and both seemed to look in unison, although not sure for what. Anna layed her head back against the rest and closed her eyes. She was tired of feeling sad. She was tired of saying goodbye.

At Dolly's, Anna sat in the cramped living room, watching a number of people act like pure idiots. A few young men were milling about and Essie and Dolly were giggling stupidly like something was funny. Anna never did get the joke, so she sat in a corner and just watched. Some different slow music played softly. Music so unlike the music from Spellman. Then one of the men mentioned getting some wine from up the way, and Essie handed him her car keys. Anna stood up.

"Essie, what are you doing?" she almost yelled. "You know I have to get back. I'll miss my train," and Essie spun and looked at her—agitated that she had confronted her in front of her friends. "Relax," she yelled back. "He'll be right back. You've got plenty of time. Quit being so blasted stiff."

"Yeah Anna," one particularly hideous idiot with a missing tooth piped up, "Stop being so stiff." They laughed at her. Anna sat back down. She felt like she did at the orphanage when she'd fought Essie down the stairs. She knew, as then, that her ears were bright red.

She waited and waited. Soon even Essie was standing by the window. Time was passing; He had not come back. Anna was mad enough to spit, and Essie knew it.

After a bit longer the door burst open and he fell in, practically blowing and huffing like the engine that Anna was about to miss.

"Essie," he sputtered pausing to catch his breath. "Your car is down the road a ways, some law man stopped it. I had come from the gin house, was headin' back here, and I was pulled to the side. I don't know why he was millin' around these parts, but anyway he was asking whose car it was.

"I said 'Essie Buchanan, Aunt Nancy's girl.' I told him we're here for your Uncle's funeral, so he let me run up here to you, but he's holdin' the car until I bring you back. Seems he needs a license or something. Do you have one? Oh, I brought your sister's things back with me."

Essie glared at him. "First off, the name's Baker, Essie Baker, and if you've lost my husband's car, he'll kill you. Second, you're an idiot. Now let's go." Then she turned to the lanky man with the toothless grin. "Take my sister Anna to the train station, in a hurry. And if you harm her in any way, I'll kill you. I swear I'll cut your throat," and he knew that she would.

Anna followed Essie outside, and they hugged closely with all too quick good-byes. There wasn't even time to cry. Anna stood awhile as her luggage and lunch were put in a dusty old heap, then waved as Essie turned around, yelling,

"Write me as soon as you get back to the home. As soon as you get home!" and Anna nodded.

They were on their way, in a car so bumpy and rickety, she felt she was riding on a camel. It was quiet. All he did was stare back and force a grin.

"His mouth looks like a fence with pickets missing," she thought as she gazed out the window. Then he spoke up, his drawl sounding like a *too slow record*. "I gotta stop to make first," he said as he pulled off on a shady side road.

Anna's heart was racing. She wasn't sure just why, but she was terrified, her mouth dry, her palms sweaty. "Where is he going, and why?" she wondered as the sorry car bumped along. "Am I ever going to make it to the station? What could be so important that he has to stop now?" she asked herself between silent prayers.

They drove a little further and now Anna's mind was also racing. The deadening silence was scary, and she was terrified of both him and this ugly car. She likened them to a creepy snake crawling, slithering through the bushes towards some unsuspecting victim. The car stopped, its destination a shanty house that she was sure had no redeeming value. It was as raggedy and ugly as both him and the car, with a couple of questionable people hanging around outside.

Opening his door and getting out, he came around to her side, instructing her that she better come inside, as she'd be far safer there than sitting in the car. Anna wondered, "Surely if the people outside look like this, could it really be any better inside?" But she didn't know. She wasn't sure of what to do, and he was starting to walk slowly up the walkway, so she got out, looking around, and followed hurriedly through the screen door, behind him.

She was right. The inside of the house was far worse. It was full of weird people she'd never hoped to meet, but who she had heard hushed whispers about. Twangy, sad music played, too loud in her ears, and the smell of rot gut liquor burned her nose. She noticed a straight back chair by the door and proceeded to sit down.

The man walked on through the house and was met by a big-hipped woman, who wore enough make-up to paint a wall. She was horrible and brash, and Anna watched intently as her loud voice lowered as she talked to the man. They whispered back and forth and drank something clear out of glass jars, as they glanced first at Anna, then at each other. Anna was horrified. Her eyes darted nervously as different people approached them, looked over at her, then walked away. Some walked upstairs hugging and drinking, the creaky steps bemoaning their usage. The two kept their distance still whispering, plotting, and Anna felt a fear she couldn't explain.

Time was passing, she knew she was going to miss her train, and suddenly the fear turned into anger. She could actually feel the heat rising to her ears, and as the two cohorts approached her, she stood up.

Facing them directly, she started to speak, clearly, sternly as a school matron, speaking to her pupils.

"My name is Anna Mae Buchanan," she started," and I'm from Spellman Seminary. I am one of Miss Chadwick's girls, and I'm not sure exactly what you're up to, but I suggest, no, I demand, that you take me to the station. Now since you've made me miss my train already, with your stupidity, you will drive me to the second stop, for it would be a shame if I don't arrive in time. My sister Essie knows who I left with, and believe me, we all know it would be a shame if Miss Chadwick had to come looking for me, now wouldn't it?"

The room was silent, and for the first time Anna looked in the woman's face. She sensed a tinge of understanding like maybe the woman had some knowledge of Miss Chadwick, and she was right.

"Take her directly to the station," she barked at the dim-witted man who just stood there. "And I mean directly to the station, so this girl can get back to school. And check back here with me as soon as you get her there," she ordered. "Besides, if there were more good school girls like her, there'd be far less women like me," and Anna could almost feel the despair in her voice. Then she touched Anna's face and they headed back out the door, past the outside side show, and on to the rusted car, that by now looked almost good.

The ride to the train's second stop seemed even quieter, and Anna felt smug and self-assured as they puttered along. It was almost dark now and she glanced quickly over at the man whose name she did not know. Then she smiled openly, staring back out the window and relishing the fact that he was no longer grinning.

Anna was relieved to be back at school, and was eager for the routine to set in. The first day back she rested mostly, for that overwhelming draining sense of fatigue just never quite seemed to leave her body. It never did, and often she wondered how much longer she would have to be on medicine. She knew she couldn't be tired from too much work, because for years her load had been cut in half. Her chores were mostly teaching, office work and supervising, but no matter how much Scott's Emulsion she swallowed, it didn't seem to be living up to its promise. Every two or three months she was seen by a doctor, but nothing was ever said to her so she figured she had little energy because she was little.

She spent a week or so, off and on, chatting with Miss Chadwick about her visit, and the woman listened to her quietly, as if trying to implant the words into her mind. Anna thought that since she'd been home, Miss Chadwick had seemed sort of distant, but she attributed it to the overwhelming burdens that she faced every day, and didn't question her. Anna loved their long talks, and Anna loved Miss Chadwick, whom she considered a very close friend. So, life went on as usual, although strained.

A couple of weeks into the next month, the girls saw a notice on the bulletin board in the hallway, saying that an assembly was to be held on the upcoming Friday in the auditorium off the stairwell. It was to start at 1:30 after lunch and the remainder of the school day would be dismissed. It didn't say why or what for and by Wednesday, the school was all a chatter as to its mystery.

Miss Chadwick was approached by several girls, even Anna, but she brushed them off, almost curtly, by changing the subject or walking away. "This must be a real surprise," they all thought. It was on Thursday, after dinner, when all was completed, Anna mailed some letters to her family back home, then went to the music room to play her songs.

As she stood by the window looking out she could hear from way across the way the faint distant wails of what she'd learned was blues music, and she sat down a moment to think of home. Soon she had put on the classics that so absorbed her, so she never heard the door open, and jumped as she opened her eyes to a small brown child who stood before her. The child handed Anna a note, and by its stationary she knew it was from Miss Chadwick. "Come to my office, whenever you're free," it read, and Anna thanked the little girl, turned off her music and started down the shiny lit hallway.

Miss Chadwick's office door was partly open, so Anna stood in the doorway, knocked softly, and waited to be asked in. Sitting behind her large polished desk, Miss Chadwick motioned and Anna entered the room, taking her seat in a tall cushioned chair directly before her.

She felt cold. All of a sudden, Anna felt cold, and dread crept from her soul as she studied the eyes of the woman who'd been crying. A short while passed, a tense awkward silence. Then Miss Chadwick started to speak.

"Anna," she spoke softly. "Do you remember when you left to go to your Uncle Mayo's funeral, and I told you that when you got back I had something to discuss with you?" Anna nodded. "Well," she continued, "as you know, throughout your many years with us you never have been well. We haven't really discussed things with you but the doctors seem to think it's because of this air or something like that, that keeps you so weak and small. I've known for quite a few years, but I always thought you'd get better. I was selfish and I couldn't bear the thought of letting you go. You're as my child. The last couple of years I've been in touch a lot with your Aunt Nancy, and even Essie, and at the doctor's insistence, we have come to a conclusion. This is your last year of schooling here, and you've been given a scholarship to another school. It's in Cheyenne, Wyoming, and you'll be living with your sister Essie from now on. Anna, it's a fine cultured school and it's a white school, but I don't see a problem for you. You can more than hold your own. Because it's in a high altitude, the doctors feel that you will fare better, be healthier, and grow. You can't even stay with your Aunt Nancy. You must go out west for your health. Besides, you saw your Aunt. She's tired, Anna, tired and sick—and she's come to a point now, that to survive, she must start taking care of herself. That just leaves Essie. She's all you have left."

There was a pause, and Anna never answered. Her face was white, and she knew that the lump in her throat was her heart. Miss Chadwick went on.

"This is the reason for the assembly tomorrow, to announce to the school your leaving. This is the reason for my quiet, my sadness, and my pain. I love you, child. Just like you were mine. And you are mine, you'll always be mine. But I have to let you go. I love you because you came here so small and alone. I love you because you excelled and made me proud to be your teacher and your friend. I love you because you somehow needed me more than the others."

Then the voice trailed off. "Dear God," the woman sobbed into her hands. "Dear Sweet Jesus," and she turned her chair slowly towards the window as if wanting to be alone with her pain.

Anna said nothing, for what was there to say? She looked down at her knuckles, which were blue from grasping the arms of the chair, and loosened her grip. She stood up, although her legs were trembling so violently she was sure they would not carry her. But they did, and she both stumbled and ran down the halls, blinded by tears that almost stung her. That's how great was her anguish. It was like someone had beat the wind out of her, and she ran into her room, gasping, reaching for her tonic, and praying silently that she was dreaming.

But she wasn't dreaming, nor did she sleep all night. Her thoughts were muddled and painful, and she knew that her life, her home, her safe haven as she knew it, was over. It was gone, and being in Cheyenne with Essie was going to be very different. If ever there was a time to grow up, Anna knew that this was it.

Anna was the last to enter the auditorium that next day, walking quickly past the other girls to take her seat in the front row. A number of people spoke about this and that, regular school news was discussed, the upcoming field trip was planned, and Anna sat numb—hearing none of it. The girls were still wondering what was the big news. Then Miss Chadwick walked stiffly to the podium. Her graying hair was perfect as a picture, her face solemn, her tone even. She spoke, her lifting diction making the words seem like a soothing song. She told them about Anna. She told them Anna's news in length, in detail, elaborating on the morals and merits of the new school. She told them that Anna would be living with Essie, who had prospered very well, and about Wyoming with the high altitude for Anna's health. She told them that Anna would be leaving in about a week. She called Anna up to address the assembly, then walked across the stage to her chair.

Anna stood up and walked to the stage. Her legs were still wobbly, and she stepped, as if in slow motion, then stood behind the wooden podium, which hid all of her body, except her head. This was one time that she was glad she had bad eyesight and could focus on no one, especially Eva and Catherine. For somehow through this long struggle they had become friends. All the ones that had caused her so much pain, or had disliked her so, were long gone, and Anna held a position of respect. The younger charges especially liked her, as she'd taught and helped them along many times. She'd miss them. She'd miss everyone, and she knew that in order to maintain some sort of composure, this was not the time for one of her long orations.

There were whispers throughout the auditorium, and even a few muffled cries, for everyone just assumed that Anna would just stay on here, and help out after graduation. Anna was glad that she could not put a face with any of the sounds.

"I'll miss you," she said softly, her trained voice loud enough to hear, but tinged with the edge of defeatism. "I'll miss you all. Today, I have no eloquent speech. I'm not even sure of what to say. All of the words I've mastered so well, throughout the years somehow do not seem appropriate now." She turned her head to Miss Chadwick, who sat properly beside Miss Sadie, Tugar, Bessie and Miss Fenicle. All older, most graying, and none returning a glance. Anna continued. "I thank you for my life, and I love you with all my heart. I'll miss you." Then she turned and left the stage, hurrying down the aisle, past the girls and the hands that reached out for her. She ran to the big tree and cried, and everyone left her alone there with her sorrow.

The week passed slowly and Anna, as she'd been taught, was packed way ahead of time, which was easy. She didn't have much to pack. Her things sat in her room in a corner by the window and no one really commented or approached her. Even the matrons were quiet. Miss Chadwick spent four of the days in town, but Anna understood. Good-byes were never easy. She had written short notes to Eva and Catherine, asking them when it was time for her to go, would they go out to the crying tree, so they wouldn't have to say goodbye. They agreed.

Miss Chadwick had taken care of the arrangements, the train tickets were purchased for a seat, right up front —still the porter and engineer were instructed to watch out for Anna. A case of Scott's Emulsion was sent ahead to Cheyenne, and a doctor was contacted there to continue her treatments. The new school was contacted—her papers, grades, merits and awards sent ahead, were waiting for her there. Essie and her husband, Philip, would pick her up at the station. She was instructed to settle in for two days, then with the money she was given to live on, buy a few clothes, and necessities. She was also given a letter to present to her new principal. Everything was done, taken care of, except the pain, the emptiness that tore at her heart.

The day came, as all days do, and again Anna found herself standing in the hallway, luggage in hand. She stood there with her head down, glancing up just briefly as Eva and Catherine hurried past her, out the door to the oak tree. All the good-byes had long been said, and surely there could be no tears left. So Anna stood there, her head down, staring at the shiny linoleum.

"Hold your head up, Anna," came the soft voice of her teacher and friend. "Hold you head up high. As I've told you, never look down, for you're one of Miss Chadwick's girls. You're special, you're proud and you have nothing in life to be ashamed of." And she held her.

Anna looked around one last time at all she had really ever known. Everyone except Miss Chadwick had scattered off when the car pulled up, but Anna was aware they were still watching. She smiled at their futile attempts at hiding, knowing they saw it. Then she and Miss Chadwick headed out the door. On the walk to the car Anna looked over at the crying tree. Eva and Catherine leaned against it, as if holding it up, hankies in hand. Anna waved, but all they could do was cry. Miss Sadie, Tugar and Bessie stood on the porch waving, and were soon joined by Miss Fenicle. "Don't forget the doilies, Anna," Miss Fenicle yelled, then scurried back in the house, followed by the other matrons.

Anna and Miss Chadwick stood by the car, their awkward silence making its roar even more obvious. Miss

Chadwick again held her, her voice barely above a whisper as she talked.

Crying softly, she cradled Anna's face in her dainty hands.

"Can you really be that small child who entered my life so many years ago? Oh, your eyes and hair are darker, and your freckles may be gone, but you're still the same to me. Now go, Anna, don't look back— we have prepared you well. Take with you all the gifts and knowledge from me, Aunt Nancy and even Lula, for all of us in our small way have tried to prepare you for this moment. The rest is up to you, for you're seventeen now, almost an adult. Just remember that good or bad, if the decisions in your life are all yours, then they are okay. It's all right. And know that I am always with you. Every time you read a book, or write an oration, or listen to the music, I'll be there. No matter which road you choose, if you're happy, then it's the right road. I want you to know that this is one of the hardest things I'll ever have to do, but keep me in your heart, Anna. You will always be in mine. It's time to go now," and Anna got in the car.

Rolling down the window, she looked for the last time at the friends that she loved so. She looked at the grounds and the trees and the chapel, and in her heart she knew that she would never see them again. Anna said nothing, there was just nothing to say, and as the car jerked to a start Miss Chadwick kissed her forehead.

"Remember," she told Anna, "hold your head high, read His word, and remember the parables. I love you," and she stepped away form the car.

"I love you too," cried Anna as the car started down the way, kicking up the dust like the doodle-bugs.

Anna got on her knees and looked out the rear window of the car. And as they drove up one small hill and down another, she watched a part of her life appear then disappear, then fade to a memory. And all of a sudden Anna knew where she'd seen those eyes. Those eyes were part of everyone who had ever loved her, of everyone who had touched her heart, of everyone she had loved.

The train ride to Cheyenne was a long one and Anna sat alone, crying without shame. Her eyes were swollen almost shut and she just didn't care. She was going to miss them all so much. Maybe things would have been better if she at least could have gone with Aunt Nancy, but because of her health she had to go to Wyoming, to live with Essie. Life with Essie—she wondered how this would be.

Essie picked her up at the station and the ride to her small house was quiet, but she understood. She knew that all of this was going to be an adjustment for Anna, and somehow she would help her fit in.

Essie's house was small but neat and they had fixed up a small room for Anna off of the living room. Anna thought that her husband Philip was a kind man, but he was so much older, and always seemed to be gone. Always ripping and runnin' and working for Essie, who continually treated him with indifference.

Anna spent most of the first two days by herself, crying and writing long letters to both Aunt Nancy and Miss Chadwick. She knew that often they would be too busy to answer all of them, but somehow it made her feel better. She was so lonely. Oh, Essie did her best, and she had lots of friends she introduced her to, but Anna knew she would never fit in. What works for one person will not necessarily work for another, and Anna felt ridiculous trying to act giddy.

The following week, Essie showed Anna the way to her new school, a red brick building named Cheyenne High, that set off to the side by itself. It wasn't to far from Essie's, but Anna still looked on it with dread. She learned early on to expect the unexpected, and she knew that being in an all white school would be challenging.

On the first day Anna went to the principals office to get a list of where she was to go. He was as kind as he had to be, but admitted he was pleased by the accolades that had preceded her from Miss Chadwick.

Finally he cleared his throat and spoke, his voice droning on like a cricket in Autumn.

"Miss Chadwick has informed me that you are an excellent straight A student and I'll expect no less of you here. She says you excel in speech or debates, which is very good as we have a big meet coming soon. She also wrote a little about your life, which will be kept strictly confidential. Now here is your list of subjects, and if there are any problems, please feel free to return to my office."

Anna sat for a moment; then, realizing the conversation was over, she thanked him, picked up her list, and headed to Room 110. A number of girls both in the hallway and the room nudged and whispered to each other, and Anna wasn't sure if it was because she was new or black. She figured she'd find that out, when she found them out. That first day seemed like an eternity, and all the days and weeks that followed were just the same.

At the house Anna did as much as she could to help out, but Essie generally ended up shooing her away, saying things could wait. There were just too many places to go and she wanted to introduce and show Anna around. And she tried, but everywhere they went Essie was the belle and Anna merely stood around like a wooden hat rack.

So Anna poured herself into her studies, ignoring those who were rude and yet leery of those who were not. She got a little job doing some light washing and ironing and babysitting for a family a few blocks away so she wouldn't have to be a burden to anyone, and continued to write her letters to her loved ones. The warm nights sitting on Essie's porch served as a constant reminder.

Cheyenne High was different, far different than Spellman had been. It was sort of stiff and rigid but the teachings were good. Anna heard about the debate the school was having and several of the girls were going to enter.

Much to the surprise of the other girls, Anna submitted her name, and much to her surprise she was chosen, but she was soon to find out why.

The class was called American Literature and the topic of the debate was, "What Have Both Black and White Americans Contributed to America and Literature?" A small thin white girl named Deloris was chosen and of course Anna was chosen because she was the only black in class. She was excited because this was an area she had full knowledge of. All she'd learned at Spellman gave her a wealth of information and she eagerly wrote her essay for the debate.

The day of the debate came and everyone sat in the assembly hall, curious how things would turn out. Deloris had a team of supporters and Anna sat alone, but she didn't mind. Deloris was a nice girl, and besides, once they got on stage they'd both be alone.

Deloris's name was called and she climbed the few steps to the stage. She started to speak, strongly, self confidently, ending with a roar of applause. "She was good, very good," Anna thought as she took her place on stage, thankful that this was just a presentation, not a contest.

Anna started her essay, drawing on everything she was taught, everything she had learned. Her voice was clear, assertive, and perfect, and she knew it. She'd long ago learned how to make it rise and fall like the tides on a windy night. They were rapt and she knew it as she told them things they'd probably never heard before. The teachers and faculty watched intently.

She told them about the heroes such as Crispus Attucks who was the first to die for our country during the Revolutionary War. She told them about Benjamin Banneker who invented the first clock to strike on the hour, and of Sojourner Truth and her fight for freedom. She told of Granville Woods and his first electric railway system. The audience was silent. Anna then turned her speech to the literary contributions, starting with poets and writers, music, spirituals and their origins. She spoke of Paul Laurence Dunbar and recited some of his poetry, "De Party," and "*When Malindy Sings*" in dialect. She ended with "*The Rose,*" in perfect dialog. First there was silence. Then there was a thunderous applause that seemed to last forever. And Anna was on top of the world, for she knew that this oration was her ticket for the ride.

School was going well, things were going well and if it wasn't for missing her loved ones, Anna could have been happy. Or maybe she was happy, but she just didn't know it. There was a tall lean boy she'd noticed, and she thought he was nice. He didn't seem at all like Essie's leering friends. He used to talk to Anna a lot and sometimes he'd drop by and sit on the porch with her.

This went on for a few months and Anna felt herself thinking about him. Essie would put make-up on her, she said to make her prettier, but Anna felt ridiculous. She just did not have the face for all this mess. It worked for Essie but not for her, and they both knew and felt like she looked like a clown.

One day a letter came from Miss Chadwick and Anna rushed to do the ironing so she could read it. She liked to have things done so she could read in peace, undisturbed. She folded the last load, ran it to the neighbors, then sat on the porch to read the note.

Dear Anna, I hope this letter finds you well, happy and thinking of us, as we are thinking of you. Everyone really misses you here Anna. I can only pray that you are adjusting well, in these few months, and from the reports I've received from Cheyenne High, you are excelling in every subject, as I knew you would. School will be over soon, and your life will be yours, and I know you will make the right choices."

Something funny happened the other day. I was standing out front and a car pulled up. A woman and a child got out and I walked over to them, to greet them. The woman was crying. She told me the child had been left with her and she could no longer take care of her. She asked if she could leave her with the school.

Well Anna, I lifted the little girls head and there you stood. Almost the same frightened face that I'd seen in you, and even though we scarcely have room, I accepted her into our home. She's a wonderful child Anna. Bright and tiny and it's almost like having you here again. She's a fast learner too."

Eva and Catherine have left Spellman, opting to live with relatives in Kansas. They wanted to start living and working on their own and they've promised to send an address when they get settled. I'll send that information on to you.

I miss you very much. I probably always will, but it's strange how life goes on. For everything we lose there is something that we gain, and I know God sees to that. Take care of yourself dear Anna. Take your medicine and know that I love you.
Miss Chadwick

Anna dropped the letter on her lap, and watched the sun as it made its descent. She felt sad inside, almost empty. "I've lost her," she thought. "I've been replaced," and she sat far into the night wondering why people had to come and go so much in her life.

Yet the boy kept coming around, and Anna was never quite sure why. She'd seen a lot of girls talk to him, but she just assumed it was because he was so nice. Besides, these were bad girls, girls that threw snide remarks at her. Girls who called her pale and stuck up. Surely a boy of his caliber could have no interest in them.

One day, while sitting on the porch, the boy asked Anna to marry him. She didn't quite know what to say, but she went ahead and said yes. For what was love? She didn't know. There were also so many unanswered questions about this person, but she figured he was just different. She felt she could trust him.

School was ending and Anna was happy to have plans to make. It filled her time and her mind. It helped her to forget. She decided she'd wait to tell Miss Chadwick and Aunt Nancy because she did not want them to try and make the burdensome trip. She wrote them and told them she had a surprise.

She hadn't seen the boy lately, but that was okay because the Saturday was already picked. They'd meet at 1:00 p.m. at the wooden church by the pond, and even though Essie kept throwing her doubts in, Anna felt in her heart that things would be okay. He came by the Friday before the wedding, but seemed like he was in a hurry, no time to talk. Anna just figured he had the next day jitters.

Saturday came and Anna wore a long beige dress with lace, that was Essie's. She trimmed up her hair, and put a flower in the side and allowed Essie to paint her face with color. At ten to one, Anna, Essie and a number of friends went over to the small church to wait. Anna went in and sat on the front pew. She could actually hear her heart beating through the lace.

One-thirty came, two o'clock, three. Anna turned to notice a lot of people had left. At four, Essie shooed off the rest and went and joined her sister on the bench.

"Let's go, Anna," she told her. "He's not coming. He's not going to show up." And she cried as she hugged Anna and picked up the daisies. But Anna did not cry. "I want to be alone for a while," Anna told her. "I'll be home in a minute, you just run along." And Essie left her sitting on the front pew, picking at the petals from a Daisy.

Anna reached and took the flowers from her hair. She laid them on the bench beside her, thinking, "Surely there's no reason for this now. It looked ridiculous anyway." She wiped the lipstick from her mouth.

She sat a bit longer, until she was sure everyone was gone, then walked out the door as the sun set. A bright orange engulfed her, and she was lost in inner thought. She wasn't hurt because he didn't show up. She figured he'd probably turn out to be an idiot anyway. She was hurt because it was just one more painful blow. Few people liked her anyway and this was really something to keep their lips a-flappin.

No, she wasn't hurt, she was mad. Madder than she'd ever been in her life so far, and if her ears were never red, they were now. So mad that she never noticed the junk heap of a car that rolled along side her. She never heard the taunts. All she wanted was to get home.

The car rolled to a stop and several people got out. "My, my, now don't you look cute," one of them flung at her. "How was the wedding?" and Anna stopped in her tracks, just now noticing their presence. Her inner voice said to keep walking, but her outer rage brought her to a stop.

Anna looked at the three girls who encircled her, laughing, jeering, and then over at the boy who leaned grinning against the dirty car. They started pushing her, but her mind was so addled she didn't feel it. She just kept her eyes on the boy who grinned like a cat eating paste. They slapped her, kicked her, called her mean, yellow and uppity, and she fought them, all of them, feeling none of the pain. He had cowered himself inside the car, and when Anna couldn't hit one of them, she hit and kicked the car trying to get at him inside. He was no longer grinning. Then Anna broke free and made a lunge for him, smashing her fist through the glass sending it spraying in a thousand different directions. She grabbed him, slapped him, scratched him, and he shifted between trying to stop her and picking the sharp glass out of his collar. The girls screamed that she was crazy as they climbed back in the car, but she didn't care. This was a rage that had built up for so many years, and she wasn't even aware that she was bleeding. Then as she dangled through the window, the car sped off leaving her alone in the dirty street.

Anna sat on the street for a moment, tying to collect her thoughts. The smell from the car's exhaust pipe stung her nose, and forced her back to reality. This was reality for her. This was it, and Anna knew exactly what she had to do.
So she stood up, rearranged the torn lace, and made her way home.

The house was empty and Anna was glad, as this gave her time to clean up both herself and her mind. Standing over the sink, she finally noticed that she'd been cut on both arms and hands from the broken glass. She poured rubbing alcohol on her cuts, wiped off the rest of the clown face and brushed the dirt and glass out of her hair. She took off the tattered dress, threw it in the trash pile, and put on a long muslin gown.

In her room, Anna piled her few belongings in a corner on top of her suitcase. She folded her hankies, counted her money, said her prayers, and thanked God for all His blessings. For the first time in her life she knew exactly what she had to do. And she dozed off to sleep, wondering what sort of fib she could tell Miss Chadwick and Aunt Nancy about "*The Surprise.*"

Anna spent most of Sunday in her room, leaving just for water, and in the early evening to see if she could help with dinner. Essie was in the kitchen, peeling boiled potatoes, while Philip sliced a brown loaf of bread. Anna was told that dinner was ready, but she declined, saying that she was not hungry.

"Philip and I are going fishing by the far pond early in the morning," Essie told her. "Would you like to join us?" Anna said no thanks. "I'm sorry about what happened with those fools, but you know me. And you also know that I can't let it end like that. I swear to you I'm going to get them all, all four of them, if it's the last thing I do."

Anna smiled, for she knew if anyone would, Essie would. Philip was just quiet. He always was, for he'd learned long ago that it did no good to dispute her.

"This wedding cake here," Essie spoke up, putting down her paring knife, and turned to face her sister. "What do you want me to do with it now?" Anna met those devilish eyes, with a sneer all her own, as she dumped it in the garbage among the potato peels.

In her room Anna set to writing letters to the people she loved best. To the only people who'd understand, and soon she had drifted off to sleep.

The next morning, Anna woke up and went in the kitchen to see Essie, but remembered that she had gone fishing. "All the better," she thought, and she ate a piece of brown bread with jam and buttermilk. She then cleaned up her mess and propped her letter to her sister against the breadbox.

She was waiting around for the mail whistle, but decided to tidy up her room first, knowing the nosy neighbor up the way would get to the mailman first. That's so she could deliver everyone's mail and know who got what.

So Anna busied herself, cleaned up both herself and her room, and soon there was a loud knock on the screen door. "That's her," thought Anna as she walked to the door with a forced smile for the meddlesome woman. By now Anna knew that the whole town knew what had happened on Saturday, and she wasn't about to go into any long explanations with this person. So she just took the two letters, thanked her politely and closed both the screen and the door, careful to wait a moment or two before peeking out. Sure enough, there the neighbor stood, all a gasp, her mouth in a drawn line, flustered because she wasn't able to wrangle any information. Anna closed the curtain.

Two letters had come, one addressed to her from Miss Chadwick, the other to both her and Essie from Mrs. Reed at the church. Opening the window in her room wide, she opened the one from Miss Chadwick.

Dear Anna, I hope this letter finds you well and in the very best of spirits. Things here are running wonderfully smooth, and I will admit that the new ward that they've brought us is a delight. She's very bright and picks up things well, although she's quite shy. Sound familiar?

I'm actually writing to tell you about Eva and Catherine. They've settled in with the relatives who had contacted us. I'm informed that Catherine will have a job of sorts with books and Eva will see to the care of an elderly relative. Both girls are quite excited and asked me to tell you of their good fortune.

I'm going to close now Anna, with I love and miss you and Essie dreadfully, and pray that you've found some semblance of happiness in your lives. Oh, and Anna, I can't wait to hear about your surprise, so write soon and take care.
Love Always,
Miss Chadwick

Anna smiled, happy that she'd already written her to tell her of her plans. Even though the other letter was addressed to both sisters, Anna figured it was all right to go ahead and open it. She couldn't imagine what Mrs. Reed could possibly want with the two of them.

Dear Nancy's Girls, Being as I didn't know how to reach you, I had to look up Dolly to get an address to send this. As you know, when you were here your Aunt wasn't too good, and I must tell you that Nancy died last week. We couldn't reach you girls 'til now and we buried her at the bottom of the hill by her brother Mayo. She's resting now.
Mrs. C. Reed.

The letter fell to the floor, and Anna collapsed on the bed. "No more, dear God, no more," she moaned, burying her face in the pillow. This pain was more than she could bear. Her sobs were uncontrolled, she made no effort to subdue them. The pain was so bad, a broken heart hurts so bad. "Dear Jesus, help me," she whispered aloud as she closed her eyes to picture her Aunt Nancy, and the eyes that she'd always loved so.

After an hour or so, Anna got up, picked up the letter and put it in the kitchen, against the breadbox alongside the one she'd left for Essie. Then she went in the room, gathered her things, and headed out the door, careful to close it securely behind her. She then put the letter to Miss Chadwick in the mailbag for posting, and headed, walking, to the train station, not looking back.

"No more," she thought numbly, as her pace quickened, mindful of a too warm sun. "No more."

At the station Anna laid down her money and asked the man how far would it take her. He slowly made his count, looked at a long schedule, then dryly told her, "Denver Colorado."

She bought a one way ticket.

Settling in the back of the almost empty train, she figured that maybe not too many people wanted to go to Denver. "All the less to contend with," she spoke almost out loud, but to no one in particular. The scenes passed the window from slow to blur, and she likened them to her thoughts for the moment. Aunt Nancy was gone. And, as in life, she'd chosen a fashion to leave that she thought would cause everyone the least pain. But it was over now, done with, and Anna whispered her goodbye to the heavens.

She thought of the eyes, the eyes of those that she had known and loved, and realized why they had all seemed so familiar. It was her. She was what they all had in common. They were the eyes of everyone who had loved her, of everyone who had taught her, of everyone who had helped her along the way. They were the eyes of the one who taught the parables that she would follow the rest of her life. "Anything worth doing is worth doing well," and, "A place for everything and everything in its place." She knew she would always live by *"Politeness is to do and say the kindest thing in the kindest way by seeing what needs to be done and do it without being told."* She'd been taught and guided well, and finally she realized that she'd never really ever been alone. For even when things were at their worst, there were always "*Those Eyes*," someone's eyes, to guide her through the storm. Anna was starting over, and she was letting go of all there was and all that had been.

The train pulled into Denver and Anna got off without a clue of where to go or what to do. She sat in the station a while, then started reading some papers and leaflets that were scattered around.

"*For Hire*," one read. "**Someone to clean rooming house for room and board, and small salary. Inquire in person.**" It listed an address on Gilpin Street, and Anna picked up her luggage and walked over to a man who drove a car for hire. "Is this enough money to get me to this address?" she asked him, and he told her it was. So she got in the car and they headed for the house on Gilpin. She wasn't sure what she'd find there, but she was confident that this was a new beginning.

The ride was pleasant, and Denver was beautiful, clear and green. Anna figured that this must be the air that Miss Chadwick had spoken of. She wondered what Essie and Miss Chadwick would think of her letters telling them of her plans, and she fingered the unmailed letter to Aunt Nancy still in her pocket. Anna resolved that she would write the two of them as soon as she was settled.

They pulled up in front of a medium sized house with shutters and a lot of windows. Some of the brick had worn away, but it was presentable enough. There was a woman standing out front and Anna approached her, asking the car to wait. Handing the woman the newspaper article, she stood stiffly as she was given the once over. Finally the woman spoke in a stern manner, "You're kinda frail, but I guess you'll do. I'll hire you. Bring your things inside." Then she turned and walked slowly into the house.

Anna raced back to the car, thanked the driver and proceeded to retrieve her things. Then something caught her eye. There were three figures walking up the street—two women with a man in the middle. The women held onto his arm, and glided in a fashion that belied feet. They were beautiful, with faces and clothes like mannequins, and the man was even prettier than they were. He was handsome, more than handsome with dark copper skin, straight black hair, and dimples every place that there could be. They held proudly to his arm, and Anna fully understood why. The trio approached her; the women with their noses in the air.

Picking up her belongings, Anna thought almost humorously to herself, "Dear Lord, what could a man like that possibly do with someone like me?" Some of the pain, some of the doubt wanted to engulf her, and she felt even plainer in their presence. But as the warm air from a slight breeze tipped the women's noses, the gentleman turned his eyes to Anna, and Anna met them. He had warm, caring, soft brown eyes, and he nodded to her as she lowered hers, and watched them walk into the building. She stood for a moment longer, regaining her composure, then followed them inside at a proper distance. Her mind was soaring as she entered into a new time, a new life, a new beginning.

She learned that his name was Buddy. Maybe he was the one who could open the doors to the fortress of her heart.

EPILOG

Anna Mae Buchannan Coleman still resides in Denver, Colorado and is 85 years young. She marrried Alonzo Ernest "Buddy" Coleman and they had nine children, Jacqueline, Lorna Jean, Alonzo Jr. (Lonnie), Nancy Catherine, Donald, Gloria, Esther, Judy, and Shirley. They were together almost 50 years until his death August 23, 1980. They are fondly know as Nanny and Bompoo by everyone.

Essie left Philip and married an Air Force man, Bobby Jackson. They lived in Seaside, California, and were together over thirty years until his death. Essie and Anna were in constant contact throughout the years, and spoke up until the day she died. Essie Jackson died February 18, 1986. She never had any children, and neither of them ever saw Doc or Roosevelt again.

Essie lived well. Bobby took good care of her, and she had travel, new cars and new homes. Anna never had those things, but she had a lot of children, a lot of love, and a lot of beautiful Christmases. She lives her life by the parables and by God's scriptures, so in essence, both Anna and Essie were rich in what mattered most to them.

Nanny and Bompoo with their nine children, both struggled and survived. They have 30 grandchildren, 45 great grandchildren, and 4 great great grandchildren. And Anna has never been alone again.

To write to the author:
Shirley Coleman-Wells
c/o Hughes Henshaw Publications
7196 West 4th Ave - Lakewood, CO 80226
Please enclose a self-addressed, stamped envelope for reply, or $1.00 to cover costs.

Mary Tuttle

Professional Free-lance Editing
Rewrite Fiction and Nonfiction
Critique or Overview
Line-by-Line Edit

Accepting Fiction and Nonfiction
Manuscripts
[No Children's Literature or Poetry]

Send inquiries to:
Mary Tuttle
c/o Hughes Henshaw Publications
7196 West Fourth Avenue
Lakewood, Colorado 80226-1642

Lauren McAdam

Specializing in children's book illustration

&

book cover design

CREATIVE ILLUSTRATIONS

SAMPLE ARTISTIC STYLES AVAILABLE ON REQUEST

WHIMSICAL, MAGICAL, FANCIFUL AND FUN

QUICK TURNAROUND

REASONABLE RATES

For professional freelance illustrations, please contact Lauren McAdam c/o:

Hughes Henshaw Publications
Graphics Dept. • (303) 237-5905 • fax: (303) 233-6545

WE LIKE TO HEAR FROM OUR READERS

Listed below you will find some of the books our company has available. Your book dealer stocks most of these books, and the Internet Book Stores stock these books. Visit our site on the Internet: http://www.hugheshenshaw.com

Hughes Henshaw Publications
7196 West Fourth Avenue
Lakewood, CO 80226-1642

TO ORDER BOOKS

If your book dealer does not have these books described of the following pages readily available, you may order them direct from the publisher.

DEAD EAGLES FLYING
by Daphna R. Moore
New Thought, Religious Controversial literature.
There is only one virtue in life—to be yourself. One of the most difficult tasks to undertake is to introduce a new idea to the world. Not just to the world, but to yourself. Throughout history, every woman or man of genius who has contributed to the good of humanity has had to contend with ridicule, ignorance and prejudice from powerful religious and political leaders, until the wisdom of their discovery became so overwhelming, conclusive and correct that those leaders of society were forced to take notice and acknowledge the insights and wisdom of those pioneers. The book is formatted in questions and answers taken from many years of Ms. Moore's facilitating seminars. Very thought provoking and controversial.
0-9617223-5-5, 200 pgs. 5 ½ x 8 ½ $17.00

NEVER A HERO
by Sidney L. Coggins
Navy Biography, Texas Biography, Depressions 1929 –Texas
Mr. Coggins' absorbing, skillfully- praised word picture account of his personal experiences through the early and mid Twentieth Century invites the reader to explore with him one of the most dramatic and challenging eras of our nation's history. Baby Boomers: This book is a wake up call to you to not let a wonderful legacy slip through your fingers. This book represents this last great romantic era of the Twenty Century. The people of the 20's, 30's and 40's struggled and prospered, loved and lost, wept and laughed and they did so in the face of hunger, deprivation and war. Cherish this time with your parents and grandparents as they share their memories of this historical time with you and your children. Tom Brokaw of NBC Nightly News says this about his book: *"every story is fascinating and inspiring."*
1-892693-00-3, 250 pgs. 5 ½ x 8 ½ , softcover $20.00

MASSAGE EXAMS, NATIONAL CERTIFICATION TEXTBOOK
by Alice Stephens, RN
Among our best selling books in our Medical Division. Updated monthly with new questions and answers given on the National Certification for therapists.
0-9617223-1-2, Spiral Bound, softcover $38.00

HOW TO PASS YOUR MASSAGE THERAPY STATE BOARD EXAMS
by Daphna R. Moore, CMT,LMT,NA
This is an excellent book for those who want to review anatomy, physiology, hydrotherapy, and muscle origins and insertions. A book most students purchase while still in school, and for those who've been out of school awhile.
0-9617223-3-9, Spiral Bound, softcover $38.00

HOW TO PASS YOUR CNA (Certified Nurse Assistants) EXAMS
by Daphna R. Moore
Our top seller in our Medical Division. Questions given on all state boards.
0-9617223-8-X , Spiral Bound, softcover $44.00

ANTHOLOGY OF POEMS: collected from contest by Publisher
0-9617223-0-4, softcover , 200 pgs. $23.00

HOW TO PUBLISH, MARKET AND DISTRIBUTE YOUR OWN BOOKS
by Daphna R. Moore
Excellent book for those who are considering *self publishing*. Ms. Moore guides the reader through the entire process.
0-961723-7-1, softcover, Spiral Bound $12.95

TO BE RELEASED IN 1999

KAOTO
by Norman D. Messenger
Kaoto is an unusual man child born in the year 1225 A.D. of the Christian calendar. Large for his age, he grows much taller than the rest of the Anasazis. An ancient crone who is the present rememberer and wise one of the people discovers him and takes him in to train him as her successor. This story covers the last fifty years before the Anasazi disappeared. **395 pgs.**
TO BE RELEASED WINTER 1999

REJECTS
by Normal D. Messenger - 380 pgs.
The earth's crust gives way as part of nature's pattern and a small portion of Colorado mountain country is all that is left of North America. This story is about nine adults, seven children and two dogs who survived and lived to start a new society. The story covers five years and instead of the usual details of their physical hardships, this story tends to deal with the emotional hardships as these people are thrown together and must learn to live with each other. Each adult person considers themselves to have been failures in their former life. Here they must each either use the talents they have or develop new ones to contribute to the community they form to make it work so they all can survive.
TO BE RELEASED SPRING 1999